P9-EAO-709

THE COMPLETE POTTER:
RAKU

DATE DUE

AP 7 '97			
MY 8 '97			
JY 7 '97			
SE 8 '98			
OC 6 '99			
NO 26 '01			
MR 12 '02			
FE 20 0			
DE 1 '04			
DE 7 '04			
GAYLORD			PRINTED IN U.S.A.

For Angela

THE COMPLETE POTTER:
RAKU

IAN BYERS

SERIES EDITOR EMMANUEL COOPER

B.T. Batsford Ltd, London

**Riverside Community College
Library**
SEP   '96   4800 Magnolia Avenue
Riverside, California 92506

TT 920 .B94 1995

Byers, Ian.

Raku

Front cover: Shallow dish by Ian Byers, 1986,
coloured glazes, 15×12 in (38×30 cm),
(photo: Pete Macertich).
Back cover: 'Symmetrical Days Landscape
Container' by Wayne Higby, 1982. $31\frac{1}{2}$ in
(80 cm) wide.

© Ian Byers 1990
First published 1990
This paperback edition first published 1995

All rights reserved. No part of this
publication may be reproduced, in any form
or by any means, without permission from
the Publisher

ISBN 0 7134 6131 4

Typeset by Servis Filmsetting Ltd
and printed in Hong Kong
for the publishers
B.T. Batsford Ltd
4 Fitzhardinge Street
London W1H 0AH

CONTENTS

PREFACE

When first asked to write a book on raku, I was apprehensive. Writing and making are such different activities, and putting the information and ideas down on paper can fix ideas or attitudes, thus 'cornering' the activity. In writing this book, this has, of course, happened, in the sense that here is all this information, which I hope will inspire and inform the reader. It will, nevertheless, have ultimately to be put to one side by a potter wishing to discover things for him or herself. This is because raku firings naturally involve risk and uncertainty. What I do hope the book will provide is some understanding of how raku has developed and also be a practical basis for personal exploration. Writing this book has opened up areas previously unknown to me and has also stimulated an awareness of how little we understand other cultures. In writing a book of this type and size, I have had to exclude or limit much material, but I hope that it may be the start of your own deeper interests and investigations. It has been for me!

CHAPTER ONE

INTRODUCING RAKU

RAKU – THE PROCESS

Raku has become popularly known in the West as a technique originating in Japan in the sixteenth century in which work is rapidly fired, and removed from the kiln when glowing hot. A more recent Western development is the placing of the glowing pot in a container with combustible materials, creating particular colours, textures, and metallic oxides. The growth of interest in raku today is probably due to its own particular features: the earthiness of smoked clay, combined with vibrant coloured glazes and the fact that work may be glazed and fired all in one day.

My first experience of raku was with a group of students during a summer school. We built a wood-fired raku kiln in an hour, packed it with bisqued and glazed work, and took out the first pieces – all in a morning. It was a group experience and had its own dynamics, with some people involving themselves in building the kiln, chopping wood or stoking, whilst others immediately took to the hazards of heat and dealing with the work after it was drawn out. Few of us had experience with wood firing, and it was a

Fig 1 *Loading the kiln*

revelation when the glazes began to melt and boil. The whole process of melting and fusing was at once clearly visible, whereas, previously, most of my work had been carried out behind closed kiln doors, with only a hope and a prayer for success.

This involvement in the firing was a new experience and it was interesting to see how the same involvement overcame some people's fears of the fire. The work was drawn out with borrowed blacksmith's tongs, and the problem of numbers of pots and people made it difficult for everyone to handle their own work, or control the cooling and reduction of pots in sawdust. Then there was the obvious need for some rhythm or timing, as the next load of work had to be set in the kiln before too much heat was lost.

The results of our labours were, in some cases, immediately exciting, with glazed surfaces flashed metallic, crazed, or blackened by smoke. Some people had made objects that vaguely resembled teabowls, and it occurred to me that we were enacting some lost or, more rightly, never-found ritual without any sense of the sort of reason or purpose which surrounded Japanese teabowls. This thought, along with the lack of control evident in the fired work, counteracted the excitement of involvement, with the result that, for the time being, I pursued raku no further.

When I came back to the process it was almost by accident. I put some low-temperature glazed tiles into a raku firing with the intention of fast-testing some bright colours. They were only lightly smoked after drawing out, and hardly affected by the sawdust (being small they had almost cooled by the time they reached it). The smoking had in some way completed the surface: there did not seem to be a top and bottom, it was an all-over effect. That seemed to me to be a great bonus, for most work fired in kilns needed to be stood on stilts, wiped clean of glaze, or have footrings. Raku seemed to allow for and even absorb scars or marks in the glaze into its nature.

The freeing of the pot from its footring liberated the front or back, or the inside and outside, of work by making them continuous surfaces. The back or underside of dishes became as important, if not more important, than the front; the outside and inside of work

Fig 2 *Firing*

Fig 3 *The work is removed with tongs*

Fig 4 *The piece surrounded by newspaper and covered in sawdust*

Fig 5 *The heat from the piece ignites the reduction materials*

Fig 6 *Starting to clean off the carbonized surface*

formed an interplay of surfaces, of which the inside was the more logical starting point, the edge a transition, and the outside spread from the inside in a fairly free, unplanned way. The post-firing reduction effect on surface and colour through timing, temperature, speed, and different reduction materials, all worked to create a balance and tension of expectation and control. I was expecting certain combinations of effects and sought them during the 'action', but was most pleased when my expectations were somewhat defeated by events.

Harvey Sadow, as one of the exhibiting artists in an exhibition called Raku and Smoke in 1984 wrote, 'Regarding the raku process in general, the ultimate surrender of control after carefully orchestrating a set of possibilities always gives the pot an opportunity to be a little better than the potter'. In my view this collaboration with fire and smoke is no easy option: it demands involvement, concentration and considerable energy. What you personally bring to the activity in the form of ideas and expectations will shape your work as much as the process, because raku firings cannot provide the answers if the questions were not there in the first place.

Some people think that raku is not 'real' ceramics. This view was perhaps generated by Leach's garden party experience of raku (*A Potter's Book*, 1973) as a social event and by the non-functional quality of much raku work, but I have never seen raku in this way.

Fig 7 Ian Byers, 'Beaked Form', 1988, burnished, lustred and smoked, 14 in (35.5 cm) long (photo: Pete Macertich)

Mass raku is a different experience, and has led to its disregard as an activity worthy of serious consideration. Most raku potters handling this physically-involving process work either by themselves or with another partner, rather like studio glass workers. This combination of talents can give an edge in terms of timing or energy which, particularly with large work, can make the difference between success and failure.

When firing, I usually like to work alone, perhaps with some help at critical points in the firing or reduction. Because it involves action, working with someone who can skirt around the danger zone (you), and be there on cue is the person to seek. In this regard timing is essential, and perhaps a developed sense of timing is a natural requisite for raku or other post-fire treatments where the work is in close and direct contact during the firing or finishing process.

As with any activity, discovery and development can become clichés. Accepting what happens or what sells best can create constant conflicts of interest to direct expression or experience. The work may need to be fired again and again in order to rediscover itself; or perhaps raku is not the way that a particular idea is best developed. It is then up to you to make the break from the process.

Most potters who have become heavily involved with raku firings have in some way extended their understanding of the process, some to the point where their work can no longer be recognized as having anything to do with the rapid fire then post-fire reduction used first by Paul Soldner. We all need different things at different times; raku work, whatever the term means to other people, will to me always at best involve directness and spontaneity in thought and action.

RAKU – THE ORIGINS

Raku teabowls first made in Kyoto, Japan, were certainly not representative of the majority of Kyoto ceramics made in the sixteenth century. They should also not be seen in complete isolation from other

Fig 8 *Saddle stirrups, inlaid with silver, 1700 (photo: courtesy of the Victoria and Albert Museum, London)*

contemporary art and craft forms. Seen alongside articles such as the intricate and highly-technical swordguards and armour (*Fig 8*), sumptuous lacquerwork (*Fig 9*), or painting (*Fig 10*), and without the onlooker having any knowledge of the social context within which they function, they can look puzzlingly crude to the Western eye. How is it that these apparently simple objects were, and still are, regarded with such respect by the Japanese? To gain insight Western attitudes must be put aside and the objects looked at more closely. The social and philosophical background out of which raku sprang, and the origins of the Japanese tea ceremony (*Cha no yu*) itself must be examined.

THE TEA CEREMONY

Japan has often looked to China for inspiration and influence in artistic and philosophical matters. Tea drinking in Japan is thought to have arrived with Zen Buddhist monks from China in the twelfth century. Tea was originally drunk on ceremonial and religious occasions, or used as medicine. The practice then spread during the next two centuries to a wider section of the population.

Japan was controlled during the fifteenth century by a military aristocracy, who combined their talents with those of artists and writers, laying down rules for tea meetings, and including tea utensils in the lists of art treasures. This was an important act because it established connoisseurship and care of such articles, and it also enhanced the cultural standing of the owners. Christine Guth, writing on Sencha and art collecting in *Chanoyu Quarterly*, says:

Since its beginnings in the 15th century, chanoyu had provided a creative setting for artistic innovation. It helped to break down social and political distinctions by encouraging interaction amongst courtiers, samurai, merchants, artists, and craftsmen. It fostered innovation in nearly every sphere of artistic production, from ceramics and lacquer, painting and calligraphy, to architecture and garden design.

Fig 9 Box and cover (wood decorated with black, gold, and silver lacquer) (photo: courtesy of the Victoria and Albert Museum, London)

The fifteenth and early sixteenth centuries were a time of great social and political upset. The old aristocratic shoguns who had ruled since the twelfth century were gradually overthrown by a new military group of non-aristocratic birth, who now assumed power. This new force, with the help of increasingly successful and wealthy merchants, brought the tea ceremony to the point where it had a positive identity of its own, with specific rules and procedures.

TEA MASTERS AND THE FIRST RAKU TEABOWLS

Sen no Rikyu (1552–1591) was a man of great artistic judgement, and one who, as a tea master, gained influence over Hideyoshi (1536–1598), one of the three great generals of the period who gradually unified the country. Under Rikyu's influence, each element of the ceremony was carefully distilled, with the purpose of creating a situation and atmosphere where spiritual self-development could take place. His extremely disciplined version of the tea ceremony was designed to appeal to all the senses and, through a quiet focusing of the mind, to achieve an ego-less state. This state of being

Fig 10 Detail from a two-leaved painted screen – tigers in a bamboo grove, painted on a silver ground, Kano school, seventeenth century (photo: courtesy of the Victoria and Albert Museum, London)

Fig 11 *Interior of the tearoom Yuin 'Further Retreat'. Believed to have been built by Sotan in 1653, this room follows the four and a half mat tearoom proportion which was Sen Rikyu's 'ideal' in size. (Photo: courtesy of Urasenke Kyoto, Japan)*

was not concerned with intellectually 'knowing' about an object, but of literally fusing with it, of 'being' the object. A poem by the eighteenth-century poet Buson (1715–83) perhaps conveys the directness, simplicity, naturalness, and one-ness at which the Zen aesthetic aimed.

> *Dew on the bramble*
> *thorns*
> *sharp white.*[1]

The teabowl, the preparation and handling of tea implements, the quiet filtered light and simplicity of the tearoom, its scents and objects, even the movements of the people participating, were essential in his form of ceremony. In this context the teabowl exists naturally and harmoniously.

Sen Rikyu must have recognized the potential of the work made by two Kyoto potters: Ameya and his wife Teirin. Ameya's work was mostly modelled roof tiles which were low fired then drawn out of the kiln whilst still red hot. Teirin made teabowls which were looked upon favourably by Rikyu. The simple rather crude appearance of their work fitted with the 'tea' aesthetic of Wabi, which, translated, can mean 'poverty'. For the same reason of unselfconscious appearance, other rugged or simple wares such as Korean rice bowls had already been

[1] Translated by Lucien Stryk and Takashi Ikemoto (*see Bibliography*)

sought out and valued for their use in the tea ceremony during the early sixteenth century.

Sen Rikyu later commissioned Chojiro (the son of Ameya and Teirin) to design and produce teabowls to his specification. Chojiro's tea wares were to find favour with Oda Obunaga, one of the great generals of the period. This acceptance of the wares by such an esteemed figure promoted the standing of Sen Rikyu and made Chojiro's teabowls highly sought after. These bowls were carved, not thrown on the wheel, and therefore great subtlety could be caught in their structure and volume and in the relationship between internal and external space. This collaboration produced many fine teabowls, some of which are today the most highly-treasured bowls in Japan. Chojiro's son Jokei was awarded great status by no less than Hideyoshi himself, who gave the family a stamp of authority carved with the symbol raku, meaning pleasure, enjoyment, at ease, and the title 'best in all the world'. This title has been passed down through succeeding generations of the family until today and, interestingly, sometimes to adopted sons who have envigorated the tradition. Some of the most famous of the line are Chojiro, Donyu, Sanyu, and Ryonu.

Fig 12 Black raku teabowl, seventeenth-century, attributed to Kōetsu (photo: courtesy of the Victoria and Albert Museum, London)

HON'AMI KŌETSU (1558–1637)

It seems that the simplicity of the technique and equipment necessary to make raku teabowls interested potters who were often artists in other fields. Hon'ami Kōetsu, who from an early age showed great artistic ability, later influenced many areas of the arts and crafts. He was a painter, calligrapher, sword connoisseur, and lacquerwork designer who also made teabowls. It is perhaps because he did not have to live from the proceeds of teabowl-making that he was able to make his own experiments with form and glaze. The teabowl shown in Fig 12, attributed to Kōetsu, has a very subtle asymmetry and appears quite different from different angles. It is trough-like, with part of the lip burred over. The lip, harsh in places, is softened by the glaze, whose tarry texture is enriched by glimpses of the gritty body where the glaze has been scraped away. The severity of many of his bowls is not typical of raku teabowls as a whole, whose variety within the discipline of teabowl-making is often considerable.

The original teabowl-makers were undoubtedly artistic innovators, and the task has been for the later generations to keep the form alive, and to avoid overt self-consciousness and stagnation within the extreme limitations. In the West during the last 20 years raku has been the scene of much technical and artistic innovation, without the restraint or even knowledge of the Japanese taste and tradition. The link between the past now exists most positively through the activity, and its effect on the work produced.

RAKU IN BRITAIN AND THE U.S.A.

Although Bernard Leach is primarily thought of as a stoneware potter, his contact with the raku process in Tokyo in 1911, at a sort of garden party, seems to have been the catalyst for his lifelong involvement in ceramics. The description of that scene in his *A Potter's Book* still conveys the excitement, immediacy, and involvement which was engendered by the experience. Although Leach later (1920–25) held open days at his pottery in England, where raku was fired, it was never to be a major activity, and it is perhaps through that vivid description that his influence on subsequent events is most felt.

A number of American potters involved themselves with raku during the 1930s and '40s. Warren Gilbertson, who studied in Japan, became an author and had a show with raku work in 1941. Hal Riegger, Jean Griffith, and F. Carlton Ball were all teachers who experimented with the process during the '40s. By the 1950s raku was becoming more popular. In 1960 Paul Soldner, having read Leach's book, began experimenting with the technique and with post-firing reduction. The following extract from Bernard Leach's *A Potter's Book* is relevant to raku's development:

Influences from alien cultures either upon art or industry must pass through an organic assimilation before they can become part and parcel of our own growth. This happens, moreover, only when they supply an inherent need, and is usually inaugurated by the enthusiasm and profound conviction of men who have themselves succeeded in making the synthesis.[1]

This statement certainly applies to Leach, but in a different way to Paul Soldner. America by 1960 had become the wealthiest nation in the world, 'a nation overwhelmed by chrome. Planned obsolescence was built into the idea of the product, and socially the fat and satisfied America of 1960 had geared itself to upward mobility.'[2] In painting, literature, and music there was a mood of innovation and chance; the secure and the familiar were the last places that many artists wanted to get to, at least in their art. Abstract Expressionism was now recognized by museums, rather than the avant-garde galleries, collectors, and critics who had promoted it. It was an art that no longer looked to Europe for standards by which to measure itself.

One of the ideas which Abstract Expressionism promoted and evolved was concerned with composition. A painting became 'an arena in which to act rather than as a space in which to reproduce or design. A painting's composition could be all over, all

[1] Bernard Leach, *A Potter's Book* p. 10
[2] Eric Goldman, *The Crucial Decade and After*

at once, an event.'[3] The pot as an event seems to have been one of Soldner's and other American potters' contributions to future developments in ceramics.

It is too easy to place artists and their work into neat categories and to see history in some sort of fixed position, because history and art change as our attitudes change. However, American art since 1960 has been characterized by a bewildering series of styles. Almost as soon as one style was accepted, it was succeeded by the next; thus Abstract Expressionism was overtaken by Pop Art, then Op Art, Happenings, Conceptual Art, and Earthworks. Whatever directions American ceramics were to take during this period were bound to be influenced not only by the ideas promoted by all the styles, but also by the effect of all that avant-garde art which pushed innovation and ideas of how art could be made and what could be art to such an extreme. In a way, all that experiment and risk-taking must have given the American ceramics world the permission to take a few for itself. Within this world raku has evolved not in isolation but as one feature of the general development of ceramics in America and increasingly the international scene.

Whilst the main thrust of Art in America in the '60s and '70s was to expand our ideas about art almost to the point where everything can now be taken in, ceramics was

[3] Harold Rosenberg, *The Tradition of the New*

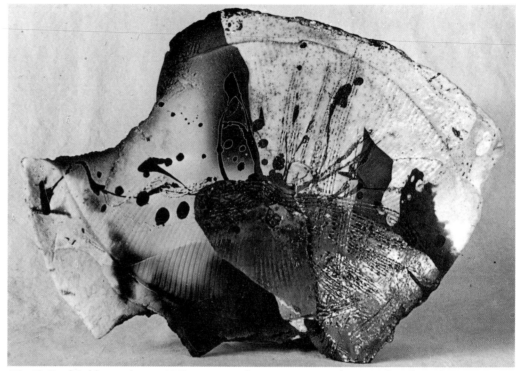

Fig 13 Paul Soldner, plaque, 1969, impressed texture, iron and copper brushwork, on top of white engobe, partially smoked. Copper glaze reduced to red. 25 in (63.5 cm) wide (photo: Ceramic Review)

not part of that vanguard, except from the point of view that making pots can be dealing with abstract form, even if it may superficially be dealing with the subject matter of the vessel. A comparison could be made perhaps with the way that Jasper Johns' flags were not the subject matter of his painting. Pot-making as a pop art also has the ability to reach large audiences.

The American ceramics of that period did, however, gain from the art scene's liberation of process, which became a valid area to explore. The idea that the art of making could have possibilities in itself, and that a piece could be about itself, is, I think, well illustrated by the Soldner plaque made in 1969, shown in Fig 13. The process of making became for some potters at times a performance enacted across the lecturing circuits of the United States. This idea of making conducted in public is still a total anathema to many British potters, and is often viewed with deep suspicion.

Paul Soldner was once quoted as saying, 'I've always liked unknown areas'. Chance was one of the means employed by artists and musicians of the period, such as John Cage, to get to the unfamiliar. Soldner, whilst working with the traditional values of asymmetric balance, used the chances thrown up by making and destroying forms during and after the throwing process. He, along with other American potters, and in particular Peter Voulkos, started to use throwing as merely the start of an idea. Voulkos was a major influence for Soldner, who says of that period at the Los Angeles Art Institute:

I thought I'd become a functional potter because that's what Voulkos was . . . he did it so beautifully. But as soon as he connected with the art school, his whole work changed. He began to use clay like any other arts medium, and I think that was a big change in clay; prior to that it was thought of as a craft. Well what we did during the next four years was just to blow that whole scene up. That school of Voulkos' was the pivotal change of ceramics in America. He was magnetic. He attracted a lot of people. It was like a new star forming.[4]

Fig 14 Paul Soldner, Bottle, 1968, post-fire smoked, wheel-thrown, approx. 18 in (46 cm) high

Fig 15 Paul Soldner, wallpiece, 'Black is beautiful', raku-fired, smoked, slips stains and clay, 23 in (58 cm) high

Forms were thrown, taken off the wheel, then recreated by another action, perhaps the only quality given to the final object being the speed and tension of the throwing process. It was an approach to throwing which embraced thickness and thinness, off-centre, asymmetry, destruction and reconstruction, with the wheel providing the jumping-off

[4] *California Living* magazine, Nov 9, 1980

Fig 16 *Paul Soldner, vessel, 1973, unglazed, low-fire salt, pink, beige and white, with iron and copper drawing. 10 in (25 cm) wide*

point for the action. This approach in Soldner's hands flowed naturally through the firing, and all the chances and discoveries of raku firings and post-fire reduction. Although not all of Soldner's work has been raku, the involvement with process during making and firing has been a continuing preoccupation.

Soldner's work has been most referential to pots, or the vessel, even when it becomes almost flat as a 'wallpiece'. It is within the area of the exploring and defining of the vessel that his work is centred, for no matter how far off he pushes, the vessel with its traditional domestic associations is there to support him.

An important contribution to British and European ceramics has been through the transfer of energy: the energy of the 'New World' to the 'Old'. This has been conveyed through slide lectures delivered by exchange lecturers from the States, or by lectures and workshops given by visiting American potters and artists. The 'go for it mentality', the enlarged scale of much of American ceramics, and the technical virtuosity shown in making equipment, which enlarged the range of possibilities for making and firing work, all had their impact.

In Britain the deluge of these visual images was greeted initially, in my experience, with mixed feelings. Innovation and experiment, obvious strainings in the direction of art, were exciting, but what about integrity, humility, and the lessons a generation of Leach and his followers had so persuasively

Fig 17 *Paul Soldner, untitled, 1984, clay, slips, salt-bisqued, 23 in (58 cm) wide*
(photo: George Erml, courtesy American Crafts Council)

Fig 18 *Paul Soldner throwing (photo:*
Ceramic Review)

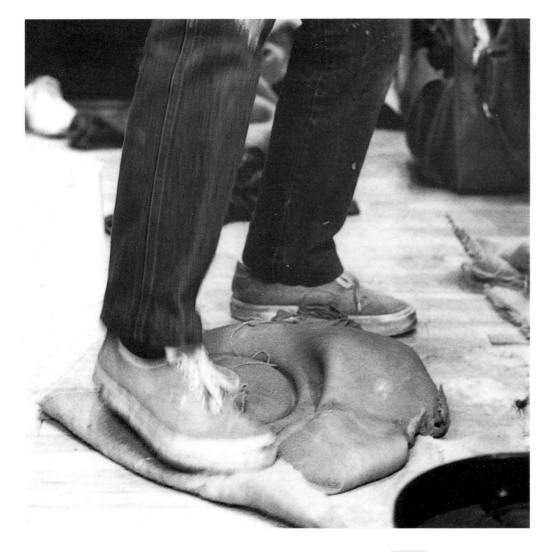

communicated? The debate about whether ceramics could be sculpture was heated, and continues to this day. There were now potters and ceramicists. The door had been pushed open and possibilities had been glimpsed which could not be shut out. The interesting thing is that few European or British potters have actually seen or felt an American pot; instead the major effect of American ceramics has been experienced through visual images and the persuasive manner and language of visiting American potters and artists.

Our age is one of instant visual communications via satellite, and we are open to the seductions of the glossy photograph. The unique ceramic vessel has been taken into the arms of the fine art gallery to be injected with credibility and status as never before. The challenge for one-off potters or ceramists is to find an individual voice. The bewildering range of traditional ceramics and the whole of art history is the background for ceramic production which is marketed with increasing sophistication.

Fig 19 Paul Soldner in action (photo: Ceramic Review)

CHAPTER TWO

RAKU CLAY AND GLAZE

RAKU CLAY

A raku clay is simply any clay which can survive the rapid heating and cooling which the process imposes, and the final arbiter over whether a clay is a success or not is yourself. Each potter sets the parameters within which he or she operates. For some, the work is small, for others large. In whatever way the work is made, i.e. slip-cast, press-moulded, coiled, or thrown, the tensions built up in the clay during making will greatly affect the performance of the clay during firing. A piece of work which has very thick and thin sections can shatter during either heating or cooling, and your control, timing, and handling of work combine with the clay's qualities to create or destroy the piece.

Many old Japanese teabowls show stress-cracks, and if bowls are broken, they are often reassembled without any loss of merit. Recently I saw a teabowl which had apparently been reassembled using pieces which were part of another bowl! I have always seen raku as being marginally functional or non-utilitarian work, except in

Fig 20 Christine Constant, slipcast and slabbed spiked cones, 1987

respect of Japanese teabowls, and therefore the fact that a piece of work cracked in the firing did not immediately pronounce it a failure. Raku is more complicated than that. The quality of a crack can actually add to the piece if the work has force and spirit. The decision in such cases is yours, but Western attitudes and ideas of perfection are not those of the East, and the people who buy your work may not be like-minded.

Anyone wishing to work in raku could best start by firing a range of different clays – some coarse, some fine, coloured or white – to see what will survive to their own satisfaction. It may be that, if you are prepared to lose work, you may gain some which has a quality which can be achieved with only a particular clay (see Fig 20). Most raku clay bodies for hand-building and throwing use high-temperature clays, such as fireclays and stonewares, as their base. At 1000°C (1830°F), and even up to 1200°C (2190°F), these clays are usually not vitrified, leaving plenty of spaces within their structure for movement during heating and cooling. To increase this openness, grog sand or even pumice may be added in amounts up to 25 per cent of the total dry weight. The particle size of the non-plastics is a personal choice, and should be thought of in aesthetic as well as practical terms. Colour is another consideration, and in the case of grog this could be made of body-stained clays, low biscuit fired, and crushed to a suitable size. The addition of non-plastics to clay results in

a loss of workability, so it is important to choose clays which are highly plastic as your starting point. This may mean using ball clays and fireclays together.

Having achieved an open texture to the clay, the further addition of materials to improve the clay's thermal shock resistance can be of help. Spodumene and talc are often added in amounts up to 15 per cent of total weight, because they help reduce the thermal expansion of the body. Any additions will, of course, change the 'feel' of the clay, and thus your response to it. If the clay is too short after mixing, plasticizing materials such as bentonite or macaloid can be added in small quantities, e.g. 1–2 per cent. All these dry materials should be dampened, then worked into the body by kneading (if adding to plastic clay). Too much water added to the non-plastics will make the clay too slippery to handle; too little will cause the clay to become too dry, short, and difficult to knead. Adding a few drops of vinegar to the water may also help by souring the clay and thus creating conditions ideal for organic life to flourish. This growth, together with the improvement in the clay's condition brought about by ageing, helps to get the best working properties from the clay (although it may give the studio a swampish air).

Making up clay bodies from powdered materials gives more choice than accepting what is available in plastic form. The dry materials should be weighed out then added to water to create a thick slip, which is then

stirred well and sieved through a 40 mesh sieve, then spread onto plaster bats to dry to a soft plastic consistency, and be kneaded ready for use, or wrapped up to age. Mechanical aids such as blungers, filter presses, pugmills, and dough mixers can both speed up the preparation and take out the hard labour from mixing large amounts of clay, but for small quantities hand methods are adequate. (Please note that it is important to wear a pottery dust mask when mixing clay powders.) Chopped nylon fibre in small amounts can be introduced into the clay at slip or plastic stage in amounts up to 0.05 per cent to help improve the wet-to-dry shrinkage of work. This also strengthens the dry clay and makes the handling of large pieces and setting in the kiln much safer. I have made up clay bodies from powders, mixed prepared bodies to obtain a composite, and simply used a specific raku body; all have their own merits which must be measured against time and cost.

At this point it is important to discuss the biscuit firing temperature in relation to types of clay. Decisions have to be made at this stage which will greatly affect the fragility and the glaze quality of the work. Some clays naturally mature at very low temperatures, and these may need to be bisqued at only 860°C (1580°F). (Fremington Red or Albany-type clay). Other clays, particularly fireclays and stonewares with grog and other non-plastics, could be fired up to 1060°C (1940°F). The more mature a body is, the less its

RAKU CLAY BODY RECIPES[1]

Jill Crowley, body for handbuilding

St Thomas's body	25
Crank mixture	75

David Miller, throwing body

Fireclay	50
Stoneware	20
Grog	25
Talc	10

Paul Soldner, salt vapour bisque bodies

Talc	20
Lincoln fireclay	50
Sand 30 mesh	30
or	
A.P. Green fireclay	40
Kentucky ball clay. OM	10

Wayne Higby, white raku body

Missouri fireclay	100
OM 4 ball clay	30
Talc	30
Silica sand	10
Macaloid	1

Red raku body

PBX fireclay	50
Gold art	20
Red art	25
Talc	5
Silica sand	10
Macaloid	1

Lila Bakke

Talc	15
Fireclay	25
Kentucky ball clay OM 4	15
Sagger clay (crank)	30
Silica sand	15
Shredded nylon	·05

Throwing body

Talc	15
A.P. Green fireclay	40
Ball clay	20
Crank	20
Silver sand	5

ADDITIONS

Oxides

Cobalt oxide	5
Iron oxide	12
Manganese oxide	10
Copper oxide	8
Chrome oxide	4
Any underglaze	8

Clay colour	Colour under alkaline/acidic glaze
Blue	D. blue/D. blue
Red-brown	D. Brown/D. Brown
Brown	Brown/Purple-brown
Buff	Turquoise/Green
Grey-green	Chrome green/Chrome green

structure will be penetrated by carbon during the post-firing process. The effect of soft glaze, such as a low-temperature high alkaline type, over a soft bisqued body can be very beautiful and is much cooler, more distant over a higher, more mature bisque surface. If you are using terra-sigillata slips, or highly-burnished surfaces, you will lose the burnished effect if you fire too high. Surface effects of clay and glaze belong to specific temperatures, and it may be that you are willing to live with fragility or lose soft qualities depending on your idea for the piece.

COLOURING CLAY BODIES

Mixing underglaze, body stains, or oxides into a clay body could be a way of linking decorating with making. If clean bright colours are required, then the body to be stained must be light coloured. Below is a list of suggested oxide and underglaze percentage additions to 100 gms of dry clay body to give a pale- to medium-strength unglazed colour. The colour can be added to the dry powdered body or kneaded into the plastic clay. If the colour is blended into dry clay, then the mixture may be slaked down with water, and sieved through an 80's mesh sieve to give a good dispersion. Grog can then be kneaded in at the plastic stage, either in a dough mixer or by hand kneading. Adding colour to clay by

[1] Recipes given in the clay and glaze sectors are expressed as parts by weight

thorough kneading gives a fairly even dispersion. As plastic clay contains water, allowance must be made for this when working from dry weight recipes. A plastic clay version of a dry weight recipe would need about 20 per cent less colour. Raku clay being low-fired, it may be uneconomic to add enough colour to make a strongly-stained clay, unless the clay is to be glazed in areas, thus deepening colours.

RAKU GLAZE

Raku glaze forms only part of the whole ceramic spectrum of colour, texture, and hardness. The band of that spectrum which contains possibilities for the raku process is constantly being widened and redefined. If we work from the idea that raku involves a particular process of firing, then anything which survives that process, whether low-fired or even stoneware, could be raku. Japanese raku has from its earliest times explored high- and low-temperature glazes, and since the adoption of raku by the West, firings have included processes such as salting, fuming, or patination, in addition to normal glaze procedures. Technically the area has stretched, been combined with other types of firing, sometimes to the point where the raku element is only a small part of the work. This chapter is therefore intended to provide a basis for personal experiment with a range of raku glaze types and qualities, which must be seen in relation to a whole work.

Glaze colour and quality are dependant upon body colour and quality. This simple, perhaps obvious, statement is particularly relevant to raku, because smoked or reduced clay can sit so well alongside glaze quality. What drew me towards raku was the wish to use bright colour and pattern, and to work over the whole surface of a piece, top and bottom, inside and out. Because I wanted bright clean colours, my first priority was to formulate or find a white body which would provide a good background to transparent colour; so although I started with the clay, body and glaze were immediately linked. The link between the two is often missed because glaze recipes are not related to a particular clay or indeed to the particular way in which the glaze is applied. Glaze recipes can at best be a starting point for personal explorations of colour and surface.

JAPANESE RAKU GLAZES

The terms red raku and black raku describe two types of raku teabowls highly favoured for use in the tea ceremony (Cha-no-yu). Red raku (Fig 21) relies for its quality and colour on the combination of an unrefined raw lead glaze over an ochreous slip. The slip is applied to the raw pot and the ware is then low-fired in a small charcoal kiln. During the firing the ware sometimes picks up carbon and other reduction marks from the charcoal, which remain visible under the transparent glaze after it has been fired (I have noticed a similar effect when overglazing a previously-reduced pot); these are considered to have great merit. So the final appearance of the ware is a combination of form, body slip, chance reduction marks, and a glaze which is transparent where thin, sometimes milky where thick. Below are three glazes of this type.

Leach raku glaze

White lead	66
Quartz	30
China clay	4

U.S.A. equivalent

White lead	60
Ferro 3124	20
Flint	20

Similar glaze using lead in fritted form

Lead sesquisilicate	75
China clay	25

Black raku (see Fig 12) is high fired to 1200°C (2190°F); not surprisingly the clay used is very coarse. The glaze contains raw lead and also a lead borax frit. The black colour was obtained from stones containing iron and manganese found in the Kamo river in Kyoto, but these are now apparently of poor quality and need supplementing with oxides. The final colour of black raku varies from a very dark treacly black or brown, to a reddish-brown, depending on how quickly the glaze is quenched in water. This type of glaze may be

Fig 21 *Red Raku teabowl, seal of Choniu, 1770,*
(photo: courtesy of the Victoria and Albert Museum, London

applied very thickly, thus changing the form of the pot. It is often pitted and bubbled, partly because of the coarseness of the clay and the glaze's thickness, and perhaps also because lead glazes tend to boil even if they are slightly reduced. Both red and black raku types of glazes containing raw lead are toxic, and this would be sensibly substituted by lead in a fritted form.

Black raku glaze

Lead sesquisilicate	45
Soft borax frit	45
China clay	10
Manganese oxide	2
Cobalt oxide	2
Iron oxide	3

FIRING RAKU GLAZES

The basic requirement for a raku glaze is that it will melt smoothly and evenly. Thickness is a factor where even smelting is concerned, particularly if uneven thicknesses occur on one piece, or if two or three pieces are being fired at once, each with differing thicknesses of glaze. It is best to fire types of glazes with similar melting characteristics or thicknesses together. It is quite possible to lose the colour from one glaze by overfiring it, whilst melting out a very thick glaze. Thickness problems can often be solved by carefully noting the temperature at which the glaze starts to melt, either by eye or with a pyrometer, and soaking the kiln at that temperature until the glaze is fully melted. Some glazes, particularly high-alkaline types, will boil vigorously as they melt out and in the process lose a lot of their bulk. If the firing temperature climbs rapidly, the glazes may continue boiling because they are now being overfired. If this is the case, dropping the temperature will suddenly produce an even surface. Lead frit glazes dislike being reduced and will boil if so treated. Direct flame-hitting work can so reduce this type of glaze that it is difficult to eradicate all the bubbles. Careful positioning of the burners and work, plus some oxidation in the latter part of the firing, should eliminate these problems.

FORMULATING RAKU GLAZES

A simple way to start finding out about glazes suitable for raku is to test fire any soft-firing frit or natural frit such as colemanite or gerstley borate. Borax frit, lead sesquisilicate frit, alkaline frit, or 50/50 combinations of each will all melt at temperatures below 1000°C (1830°F) and provide a variety of possibilities for colour and surface quality. Flint is often added to the fritted base to increase hardness, and a small amount of clay will stiffen the glaze and improve its flotation. Zinc oxide is also a useful auxiliary flux to promote even melting. Finally, the addition of a proprietary glaze suspender or bentonite and 0.05 per cent addition of calcium chloride will prevent rapid settling – a feature of many fritted glazes.

GLAZE RECIPES 960°–1000°C (1760°–1830°F)[1]

[1] All recipes shown as parts by weight

Rick Foris, crackle white

Gerstley borate	45
Custer feldspar	35

Paul Soldner

Gerstley borate	80
Feldspar	20

Gerstley borate	1
Borax	1
China clay	1

John Chalke

Lead sesquisilicate	50
Soft borax frit	50
Tin oxide	4
Bentonite	4

Harold McWhinnie

Calcium borate frit	80
Nepheline syenite	20
China clay	5
Tin oxide	1

SEVEN RECIPES USING OTHER COMBINATIONS OF MATERIALS

Calcium borate frit	53
Lithium carbonate	22
Nepheline syenite	25

High-alkaline frit	80
Nepheline syenite	20
China clay	5
Bentonite	5

Borax frit	85
Whiting	5
China clay	5

Lead sesquisilicate	50
Borax frit	30
Flint	15
Nepheline syenite	5

Soft borax frit	85
China clay	15

Calcium borate frit	40
Borax frit	40
China clay	15
Tin oxide	5

Lead sesquisilicate	70
Cornish stone	20
Ball clay	10

CHAPTER THREE

METHODS AND MATERIALS FOR DECORATION

Decoration is not extra or superfluous to form or idea. The integration and interaction of surface, whether it be texture, slips, or glazes, with the form is the mark of success. Good decoration can be elaborate or the merest touch of slip or glaze against the clay. At the same time as achieving integration with form, surface treatments, patterns, etc. can add another dimension or idea, or build another structure into the work.

To attempt the task of describing all possible methods of decoration within the area of raku firings would be prohibitive, because most techniques usable in other types of firings could be adapted for raku. Here I want to give practical descriptions of methods, together with visual images which give a sense of the quality of some methods of decoration.

Fig 22 *Ian Byers, detail of underglaze and coloured glaze decoration*

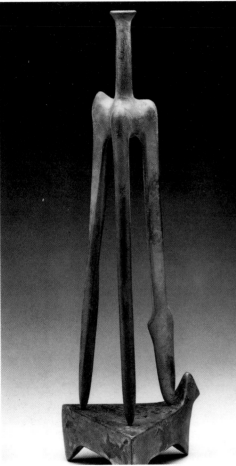

Fig 23 *Richard Hirsch, vessel and stand (Coper Metti series) 25 in (63.5 cm) high*

EGYPTIAN PASTE

This interesting material used by the ancient Egyptians to make beads, amulets, etc. is really a self-glazing clay. The open, non-plastic clay mixture has soluble salts in its make-up which during drying migrate to the surface of the clay, forming a crystal coating on the surface of the work which, on firing, forms a glazed surface.

PREPARATION

The dry ingredients are mixed and crushed in a mortar. Dry sieving through a 60's mesh sieve, whilst wearing a suitable mask, will blend all the ingredients further. Small amounts of water are then added to make a stiff dough consistency. Coloured clays must be kept damp in plastic bags or jars until used; and, once the paste is formed, either by hand or in small moulds, it should be left untouched to form its crystalline surface. A typical recipe is shown below with suggested oxide additions.

Sylvia Hyman recipe *(Orton Cone 012 (884°C))*

		or		
Nepheline syenite	39		Feldspar	34
China clay	6		Quartz	34
Ball clay	6		China clay	5
Flint	37		Soda ash	5
Sodium bicarbonate	6		Sodium bicarbonate	5
Soda ash	6		Bentonite	4
Bentonite	2			

Colour additions to basic paste

Turquoise	2.0 (red reduced)
Blue	0.5 Cobalt carbonate
Green	0.5 Chromium oxide
Yellow	5.0 Uranium oxide
Any underglaze	5.0 To give a strong colour

The oxidized colours of Egyptian paste recipes are bright. Smoking and post-reduction have the effect of softening colour and producing all the subtleties characteristic of raku, including crazing.

COLOURING SLIPS AND ENGOBES

Coloured slips can be based on a sieved version of the body used for building, or a 50/50 ball clay/china clay mixture. The amounts of colour needed to achieve a medium stain will be the same as described for clay colouring. Slips used under a high-alkaline glaze can flake off after firing because of the contraction of the glaze. This may be cured by the addition of about 12 per cent of a soft alkaline or lead frit to the slip recipe.

White engobe recipe used by Gretchen Wachs

E.P. kaolin	580	cone 06
Ball clay	400	
Cornish stone	400	
Flint	500	

Ferro frit 3124	240
Tin oxide	100
Colemanite or gerstley borate	150

(See Gretchen Wach's work on p. 33)

BURNISHING SLIPS

Coloured slips for burnishing effects may be prepared using the following recipe: 4 parts white ball clay to 3 parts underglaze or oxide colour. If the slip base is ball-milled, or if a suitable white firing clay which retains a good burnish is used, a range of colours can be obtained which respond well to smoking, giving black through to grey and finally the slip colour, when variably smoked. Black slip is obtained by adding just enough clay to either black underglaze or a mixture of cobalt oxide and iron oxide. Sufficient clay is needed to bind the pigment together. The burnished surface is an ancient way of achieving a dense coating on unglazed ware and, if the clay slip is suitable, is achieved simply by polishing with a metal spoon, smooth pebble, piece of glass, etc. Potters have their own preference for a particular tool, and each tool will impart a unique series of subtle marks to the final surface. In order to get a high polish on the finished piece, it is important to burnish at the point when the clay will squeak under the finger rather than pull. If burnished too soon the colours smear together, and if too late a good polish is not achieved. Very thick shapes are difficult to burnish, because the

Fig 24 Judy Trim, lotus bottle, T material body, coloured slip, burnished and smoked (photo: Bryan Rybolt)

thick form brings more moisture to the surface and thus rearranges the burnish. Timing is certainly critical, and the technique requires patience (*see p. 67*).

SELF-BURNISHING SLIPS

Traditionally this type of slip was used on Greek black and red wares. The slip is composed of ultra-fine particles of clay and is prepared by ball-milling or by levigation. White firing ball clays are the most suitable for the base if clean colour is required and, being secondary clays, they generally have fine particles. If slips are prepared by milling, then a batch can be made up which is then divided for colour addition. A small amount of Calgon or soda ash added to the slip will hold the particles of the batch slip in suspension after milling and will enable the major part to be syphoned off after 24 hours standing. The Calgon also aids brush application by making the slip flow better. After milling and decanting, the slip can be coloured with oxides or underglaze colours to the required strength. It may help with some colours to grind and sieve them through a 200 mesh sieve if the colours are coarse. The slips are applied thinly to leather-hard work and polished with a soft cloth when almost dry.

LEVIGATED SLIPS

Separating off the fine particles of slip by levigation alone is more lengthy. The idea is the same as the previous method – that of separating off the finest clay particles – and the method is as follows. Water is added to the dry clay to make a watery slip; a ratio of 3 parts clay to 7 parts water by weight is normal. To this slip is added a small amount of Calgon (1½ per cent of the total batch). The mixture is then stirred and left to stand for several days until the heavier particles settle out. Using a tall vessel may take longer. The top half of the slip is then siphoned off, stirred and left to stand once more, and this process is repeated until the clay stays in suspension, leaving you with clay particles of colloidal size. Some of the water is then evaporated off to bring the slip to a thin painting consistency.

RICHARD HIRSCH TERRA SIGILLATA RECIPES

Red terra sigillata

Ball clay	50 gms (17½ oz)
Red iron oxide	50 gms (17½ oz)
Calgon	5 gms (⅕ oz)
Water	400 ml (13½ fl oz)

White sigillata

Ball clay (OM 4)	200 gms (7 oz)
Calgon	10 gms (⅖ oz)
Water	800 ml (27 fl oz)

Whether burnished or self-burnishing slips are used, the possibility of contrasting shiny fine clay slip surfaces against the coarseness of raku clay is an exciting area to work in, particularly if work is post-reduction fired. Although the bottle by Judy Trim shown in Fig 24 is not raku, the procedure that she has used for smoking work produces sawdust smoking effects, with the same qualities as post-fire smoked raku.

CRAZED SLIPS

If the shrinkage of a slip is dramatically more than that of the clay body to which it is applied then it will crack and craze. The effect can also be induced by using a high-alkaline glaze over a slip. This causes the underlying slip to flake off. If the surface of work is smoked after withdrawal from the kiln, then carbon penetrates the cracks in the glaze and slip to form a sort of stencil of carbon lines on the clay surface which are revealed when the slip is flaked off. A china clay/flint slip mix will enable all of the slip to be flaked off, leaving the pattern of carbon craze marks against the body colour. A mixture of 3 parts china clay to 2 parts flint by volume will have this effect, with the added help of a crackle glaze.

Dave Roberts uses the body crackle effect to recognize the different parts of his hand-built coiled forms. His bowls often have a crazed glaze interior. This has the effect of giving density to the centre, earth-bound part of the form, while crazed slips provide larger-scale patterning works on the opening expansive rims. (See page 77 for an example of his crackle glaze.) Dave has also brought a third factor into play on some bowls by using the crackle slip loaded with copper. The slip is thickly applied to the biscuit pot and the slip surface then thinly coated with a transparent glaze.

Copper resist slip fired to 1015°C (1859°F)

China clay	85
Copper oxide	15

Transparent glaze

Soft borax frit	85
China clay	15

When the copper slip and glaze have been reduced in sawdust or straw, the slip and glaze can be peeled away. Carbon penetrates the crazing and pinholing of the coating and the copper in the slip fumes onto the clay surface, leaving subtle green, pink, and yellow markings.

COPPER SLIPS AND FINISHES

Copper slips and other metallic salts of copper have been used extensively in firings such as raku, low-fire salt, sawdust firings, and pit firings. Copper mixtures are even blow torched after firings. The main reason for using copper is its ability to produce a

Gretchen Wachs, 'Angular Series', 27 in (68.5 cm) high (photo: Lynne Lown)

variety of colours and qualities, often with unpredictable results. Several raku potters of whom Paul Soldner was the first, have used copper effects in slips. If copper slip is used in conjuction with a raku talc body and a low-temperature salt firing, subtle browns, greens,

Paul Soldner, untitled, low-fire salt, unglazed

oranges, yellows, and reddish-pinks can be produced. Some of Soldner's work has also combined post-firing raku effects with low salt firings. David Miller, who has worked extensively with salt and copper slips, uses the following slip recipe:

Boro-calcite frit	6
Alkaline frit	1
Flint	20
China clay	40
Copper carbonate	2–3

The slip made up in a thin milky consistency has to be applied thinly. Overlapping applications of the slip by either dipping, spraying, or ladling can give a rich range of colours. Salt is used during firing to bring out and enrich colours in the slip. Work can be stacked up in the kiln, with heavier work placed at the base, and space allowed for the passage of flame, and salt placed between the pieces. Salt and copper in small paper packets is placed so that it will fall onto the work during firing causing pinkish haloes where the salt touches. David Miller has described the salt firing as a 'battlefield where body and slip fight the imposition of salt, because of the high content of talc in the clay'. The amount of salt is critical – too much causing pooling inside the work, or making work stick to shelves.

The atmosphere of the kiln is best slightly reducing, and a long flame will spread the effects through the kiln. The kiln should be 'clamped' or closed up till it drops below red

David Miller, detail of slab plate

heat, when it can be opened up and work taken out to be smoked or reduced in sawdust or paper to create a further layer of effects. An over-use of salt in low firings can cause work to shatter some time after firing, as soluble salts expand whilst taking on moisture. Combining low-fire salt and raku obviously needs a site where fumes and

smoke will be dissipated without offence or health hazard. David Miller's recent work (*see Fig 58*) has moved away from use of salt, but continues to use the copper halo effect, combined with brightly-coloured stains and engobes.

COPPER MATT SURFACES

In the spectacular effects' league, the copper matt must be king (or queen). Copper carbonate or oxide is bound together by the addition of a small amount of frit. This mixture, when fired and reduced in the raku manner, can yield a brilliant range of colours in seemingly infinite variety. The effect is in a way like heating copper itself. As you watch the surface with flames licking over, colours ebb and flow as parts of the surface oxidize or reduce. The effects are elusive; even potters who have used the effect over a long period, such as Rick Foris (*see pp. 36 and 40*), may rely in some part on intuition rather than logical control.

The surface seems to need a heavy reduction of the copper surface to a bright metal before the other colours can develop. The development of varied colour is aided by turning the work whilst flames lick around it, or by the use of a blowtorch and wet cloth to freeze the effects as they appear. The surface of the copper matt has a strange velvet look, slightly granular, perhaps because of the granular nature of the copper. Possibly because of the conductivity of copper,

variables in thickness of work, and the copper application, will affect colour development and control. Different materials for post-firing reduction will also modify colour. The proportion of 90 parts copper to 10 parts high-alkaline frit is suggested as a starting point for experiment, to which small amounts of other oxides such as iron oxide and cobalt oxide can be added. The mixture can be brushed or dipped, but spraying seems to be the most effective. The work can be removed at 1000°C (1830°F), at which point the surface is mature. A glaze which matures at this temperature will give a good guide to the best time for removal.

Rick Foris, vessel, 1987, matt lustre, 17 in (43 cm) high, 1987

COPPER AND IRON MIXTURES

In the late '60s Paul Soldner used a copper and iron mixture brushwork on his work to great effect. Post-raku fire smoking produced dramatic haloes around areas of the oxide mix. The effect, like the more recent copper matt, eluded control for several years, until he realized that it relied on a reoxidation period after heavy reduction. The development of the halo was, he concluded, due to reduced copper conducting heat away from the pot to the extremities of a shape or mark, thus burning away the carbon at that point by the creation of a hot spot. The oxide mixture itself often reduces to a dry reddish pigment unless overglazed, where it may turn green. Fig 14 shows a Soldner pot from 1968 with haloed copper/iron brushwork.

SOLUBLE COPPER

Although most metallic colouring oxides are insoluble, which makes them easier and safer to handle, soluble versions offer other possibilities. Copper sulphate, a soluble form of copper, is used by some potters soaked into sawdust to create effects on the surface of pots through transference during post-firing reduction, or in pit firings. The fact that the sawdust is damp does not stop it burning and indeed aids the release of other soluble materials in the wood. Shavings or other coarse material can transfer textured marks and colour to the surface of the work, and, because they contain copper, create green-tinged haloes around the marks. It is important to note that soluble colours are poisonous and can be absorbed through the skin. Precautions should be taken when handling, preparing, or spraying colours.

COLOURING GLAZES

Any low-temperature glaze can be stained up by the addition of oxides, underglaze colours, or stains. Colours will differ between alkaline and acidic glazes, such as high-alkaline frit glazes and lead frit-based glazes. Reduction rather than oxidation will also affect the colour of many glazes, e.g. copper in an alkaline base gives red to copper metal finish when reduced, but turquoise where oxidized. Below are some basic colour additions to a high-alkaline glaze. Overfiring will often fade bright colour.

Base glaze 960°C (1760°F)

High-alkaline frit	80
Whiting	8
Ball clay	4
Zinc oxide	4
Glaze suspender	4

Colour additions to alkaline base

White	8.0 Tin oxide or zirconium silicate
Turquoise	2.5 Copper carbonate (red or metallic reduced)
Green	0.5 Chrome oxide
Blue-black lustre	3.0 Cobalt oxide, 3.0 Red iron oxide, 4.0 Copper carbonate (lustre when reduced)
Purple-brown	2.0 Manganese dioxide, 0.5 Cobalt carbonate
Yellow	1.0 Silver nitrate (oxidized)

INGLAZE LUSTRES

Lustre glazes of this type contain soluble salts of silver, copper, bismuth, and even gold. These soluble colours, together with the help of another material – soda ash – migrate to the surface of a glaze coating as the glaze dries. The thin film of material stays on the surface of the melted glaze during firing and will, upon reduction, either in the kiln or in post-firing reduction, produce lustrous surfaces. Fairly heavy reduction is required to achieve strong lustre effects, and this is most easily done in sawdust. Although the use of precious metals may seem rather expensive, amounts as small as 1 per cent can yield good results. Below are listed some starting points for exploration, using the glaze base used previously for colouring, and adding the following;

For gold lustre add
1 Bismuth subnitrate
1 Soda ash

For gold/silver lustre add
1 Silver nitrate
1 Soda ash
1 Bismuth subnitrate

For silver/blue lustre add
1 Silver nitrate
1 Bismuth subnitrate
1 Soda ash
0.5 Cobalt carbonate
The large bowl shown in Fig 26 is painted with slips and lustre glazes.

GLAZE CRAYONS

Making a glaze crayon from glaze plus candle wax offers the possibility of lines or areas of glaze which have a wax crayon quality. The idea can also be adapted for underglaze or oxide colours. The dry glaze is first sieved (1.7 oz (50 gm) will make several crayons). Paper tubes are then rolled up to the size of the crayon required. These can be set in a pad of clay ready to receive the wax mixture. First melt down the candle wax in a saucepan, taking care not to overheat it. Once the wax is melted the glaze can be added and the mixture stirred well. The blended wax and glaze is then poured into the tubes and left to set. The idea is to get as much glaze and as little wax into the crayon as possible, but a starting point for trials could be 50/50 glaze and wax. Copper glazes made up as crayons give a broken lustred line when reduced.

CRACKLE GLAZES

When a glaze shrinks more than the clay body it covers, cracking or crazing occurs. This effect has been used decoratively in the past by the Chinese in high-feldspathic glazes.

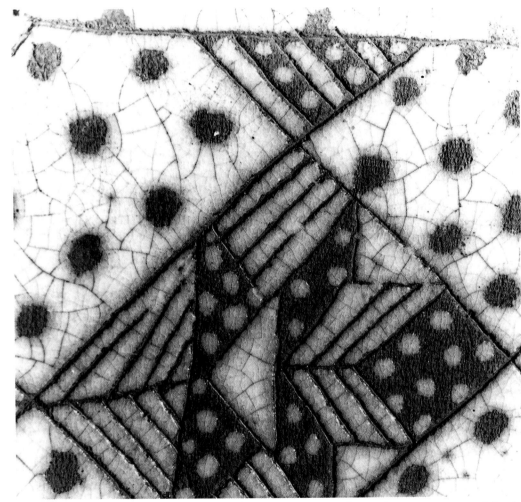

Fig 25 *Detail showing primary and secondary crazing (note relationship to wax-resisted dots)*

This crazing also occurs at lower temperatures, and particularly in raku firings, where the rapid cooling of glaze over highly-grogged bodies allows carbon to penetrate cracks during post-fire reduction. Alkaline glazes have a high contraction on cooling and will nearly always craze. However, this is not always apparent until close inspection if the glaze was not reduced.

SIZE AND TYPE OF CRACKLE

Different types of glaze will craze differently. Even lead frit glazes that are relatively elastic will craze over grogged bodies. Lead frit glazes often craze in an unpredictable way, whereas glazes high in alkalines craze in a more regular fashion. When glazes first craze, the lines thus formed are called primary crazing. As the glaze continues to shrink, secondary crazing takes place within the first craze pattern (*see Fig 25*). Because of the time lapse between the two events, it is possible to emphasize just the primary or both patterns by reducing at the correct time. As the glaze contracts, it can be heard to ping and chink. Wiping or spraying part of the surface will cause that part to craze more quickly than the rest, producing perhaps a patch of dense crackle on one part of the surface. Changing the glaze components or adding refractory colours or opacifiers may also change the character of crazing. Shown below are two of

Dave Roberts' recipes for glazes which produce different sizes of crackle.

Crackle white (large craze)

Calcium borate frit	40
Borax frit 2955 (Potterycrafts)	40
China clay	15
Tin oxide	5

Crackle white (finer crazing)

High alkaline frit	80
China clay	15
Tin oxide	5

The ability to control crazing to some degree, by the choice of glaze and by varying the cooling and reducing of glazes, allows for the development of scale and quality of crackle in relation to the size and quality of work. For example, a large craze on a small piece can be quite dramatic, whereas the same craze on a larger piece could become a subtle texture. Crazing over slip/body texture or underglaze patterns or marks can create another layer of marks, giving depth to the final idea or surface. Even resisting areas of glaze can cause particular sorts of crazing, as in Fig 25, where the crazing radiates from the wax resist dots on the clay surface.

STAINING CRAZE MARKS

If a raku-fired crazed piece is heated up to 200°C (392°F), coloured inks or vegetable dyes, etc. can be painted or rubbed into the craze lines. An alternative is to use enamels or underglaze colours which may be fixed by refiring the piece. This can produce soft crackle lines, which may be overlain with a new set of craze pattern on re-reduction.

CRACKLE AND FORM

Form will also influence how a glaze crazes. Edges or extremities will cool and contract faster than inner sections, and enclosed forms will retain heat longer. One of the satisfying aspects of some crazing is how it changes and can often relate naturally to a form. Getting to know one glaze's crazing characteristics may yield the knowledge and balance of control/non-control necessary to make crazing integral to the form.

ONGLAZE ENAMELS AND LUSTRES

Raku glazes can be overpainted etc. with manufactured onglaze enamels or lustres. Because the maturing range of these colours is above the softening point of the glaze (about 740°C [1364°F]), they may melt into the surface of the glaze or break into fragments, as in Fig 26, where the gold lustre has separated as the glaze flowed slightly. On-glaze enamels are really low-temperature glazes. They can be purchased as powders and are then prepared for painting by being mixed with either water or fat oil (condensed pure turpentine), or they can be bought in

Rick Foris, vessel, 1987, matt lustre, 9 in (30 cm) high, 1987

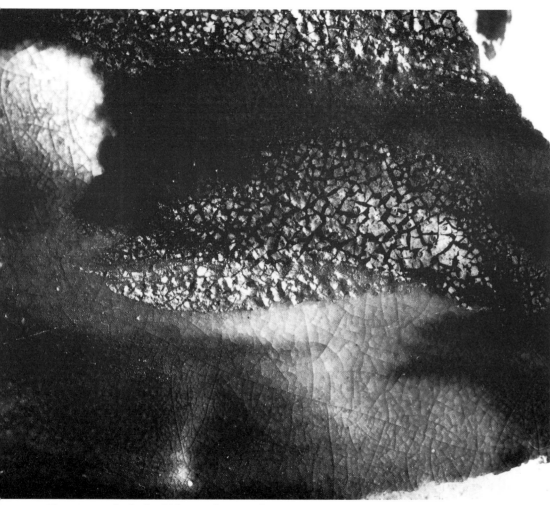

Fig 26 Detail of of gold lustre showing fragmentation

ready-to-use tube form. Industrially-made lustres are purchased ready to paint onto glaze or even burnished clay, where they may need several layers to build up a metallic iridescent surface (*see Fig 27*).

FUMING AND IRIDIZING

Fumed and iridized effects have long been used on glass, particularly on Tiffany and Carder glasses. The iridescence is produced when metallic chlorides attack the surface of a glass or glaze, to produce a refractive effect like a rainbow or butterfly's wing. The chemicals used are not only soluble and poisonous, but also corrosive to most metals. For this reason great care should be exercised in their preparation and use. Glass workers using the chemicals employ extraction equipment when spraying work and also above kilns to draw off fumes from flues. Given that suitable precautions are taken to avoid the hazards, raku work can be fumed with chemicals before post-firing reduction.

FUMING

The chemicals for fuming can be added to the kiln chamber at dull red heat, either by placing the crystals of chlorides near to the ware with a metal spoon wired to a steel rod, or by setting crystals on a brick in the flamepath of the burner. Fuming inside an electric kiln will cause rapid deterioration of kiln elements, and is not recommended unless a suitable muffle and extraction can be

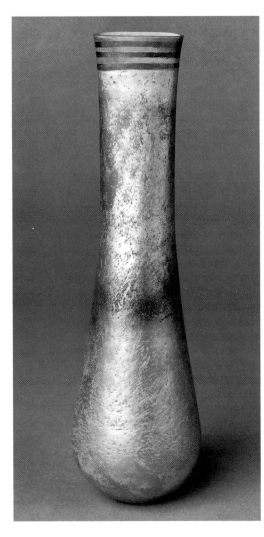

arranged. Glazed surfaces which have been lustred with industrial lustres, such as gold, copper, and silver, can give interesting results if they are fumed after the kiln has reached lustre temperature. It may also be possible to fume inglaze lustres before post-fire reduction.

Another method of attacking the surface with the chlorides is to spray the work with a chloride solution when it is pulled out. As chlorides attack metal, a spray must be found which is easily replaceable; a fixative spray linked to a small compressor is probably the best answer. Only small quantities of fuming agents need to be used, and some of the chemicals which can be used are tin chloride, iron chloride, silver chloride, titanium chloride, and vanadium tetrachloride. Three fuming mixtures are shown below. The solution strengths are 75 grams of metallic chloride to 1 pint of water. Recipes are shown as parts by volume.

Gold

Ferric chloride	1
Tin chloride	1

Silver/Gold

Iron chloride	1
Silver chloride	1

Rainbow lustre
Tin chloride solution

Fig 27 *Judy Trim, burnished, lustred flask, and smoked flask, 1984 (photo: Bryan Rybolt)*

POST-FIRING TREATMENTS

All natural and manufactured materials used to smoke work have their individual characteristics. Some contain oils, tars, and resins, some burn fiercely, whilst others merely smoulder. During combustion gases are released and ashes brought into contact with surfaces. It is therefore not surprising that the choice of combustion materials can be critical for the development of certain colours or effects.

POST-FIRING REDUCTION

When glazes are taken from the kiln glowing red hot, the glazes are still soft and molten. If the glazed object is gripped with tongs, marks may be left on the surface of the glaze. Work which is immediately put into sawdust or wood chippings sometimes bears the texture of the material in which it is placed. As the reducing materials burn, the metallic oxides in the glaze, slip, and pigments are robbed of oxygen, producing effects and colours which vary according to how long the work is exposed, the quality and quantity of reduction material, and whether the work is left to reoxidize as it cools. The variables are many, but with experience a degree of control can be achieved. It is very much a 'try it and see' experience, until some personal decisions can be made concerning the particular combination of qualities which suit your idea. Even after deciding what you think the work needs, the shape of the piece, temperature, wind, and even your speed of reaction will vary, and it is up to you to get a feel for what is 'happening' on that day. Firing a simple piece first is a way of getting a feel of the kiln and allows you to warm up mentally and physically.

REDUCTION MATERIALS

The list of materials shown is by no means a complete list of all the combustibles which can be used for reducing and smoking. It is, however, intended to provide some starting points. Materials can also be combined or soaked in soluble oxides. Simplicity is probably a good word to have in mind whilst experimenting, as starting with complicated mixtures of materials will make it hard to deduce what are the controlling factors around the surface you have just produced.

paper (different types)	shavings
sawdust (hardwood/softwood)	seeds
grass	leaves
pine needles	straw
cloth	oil
cattle feed	cuttings

REDUCTION CHAMBERS

Raku-fired work can be reduced or smoked in metal containers such as dustbins, old oil drums, or in metal boxes specially made for the purpose. These have the advantage of being portable, but metal dustbins and oil drums have the disadvantage of being usually too deep, unless tall work is being reduced. I favour either brick boxes, or lidded pits dug into the ground. Brick chambers can be enlarged or reduced in size to suit the work, and it is often easier to see the work, to cover or uncover parts of the surface, in order to allow cooling or crazing to occur. A small piece at the bottom of a dustbin which is billowing with smoke and flame is on its own. Lids for pits and brick boxes may be made from thin sheet steel and fitted with wire handles, or bricks can be built around a metal lid to form a round chamber (*see Fig 5*).

For large work it may be necessary to construct a metal box or metal mesh structure lined with ceramic fibre to slow the cooling rate and thus avoid the shattering of work. If a fibre top hat kiln is used, the top hat may be replaced with a metal tube lifted into position after the kiln has reached temperature. Sawdust etc. can then be poured around the piece with the work *in situ*. A fibre-based kiln will lose its heat easily and the heat from shelves and work will not prove too much of a hazard.

SMOKING

Exposing the surface of low-fired work to smoke and flame causes carbon to be trapped in the open pores of the clay. This smoking or carbonization becomes a permanent feature unless the piece is refired above 500°C (932°F) in an oxidizing firing. When sawdust or other reducing materials burn they produce carbon particles. Some materials produce relatively large particles whilst others release very fine carbon. Very porous work will smoke most heavily, while higher-fired work will only be greyed by heavy reduction. Smoking work with one material then another can build up subtle layers of different smoke patterns or marks which may produce depth of surface and partially, or sometimes completely, hide painted slips or engobes. Judy Trim has used smoking and the element of chance to enrich, mystify, and modulate, slip-painted, burnished, or lustred work (*see Figs 24, 27, and page 67*). Although her work is not strictly raku, it falls under the heading of, 'drawing pots from the kiln and then doing something to them' (Dave Roberts' view of raku). She says 'since my coiling method is so controlled, I especially enjoy abandoning the pieces to the risks and spontaneous effects of the firings (post-firing). Controlled spontaneity – admittedly, as I have found ways of ensuring that the smoking occurs only on the areas chosen, either by only burying half the piece, or by a pyromaniacal and frenzied withdrawal of the pot from the fire at a certain moment'.

During the smoking process, part of the work can become hot enough to burn off carbon and thus to show the unsmoked body once more. Smoking may be achieved with only a few sheets of newspaper inside a smoking pit or box. Keeping the work away from direct flame by standing it above the flame could save breakages, as subjecting work to large variations in temperature is always risky.

The effects of carbon on a surface are subtle and various. Some types of newsprint will smoke work more easily than others, because of the volatiles released from burning inks. Siddig el Nigoumi, who is well known for his burnished and smoked work, swears by the cheap tabloid newspapers for the richest effects!

It is also possible to smoke work as the kiln loses temperature by introducing carbonaceous material into the kiln itself. The Japanese have a technique called 'black fire' which uses in-kiln reduction to produce intensely-smoked surfaces. The Japanese potter sculptor Kazuo Yagi (*see Fig 28*) liked the rich surface and the control that was possible with this technique. Reducing work after a fast firing, as the kiln is cooling, is a way of lessening the thermal shock exposure experienced when moving the work from kiln to reduction chamber.

In 'black fire' firings, reduction takes place as the kiln drops to 600°C (1112°F), and is effected by introducing carbonizing materials, sometimes soaked in water, into the kiln. The kiln is sealed tightly during this procedure, and the steam produced forces the carbon deeply into the surface of the clay. The materials most used for reduction are pine needles, rubber tyres, and mothballs. Experiment, inspiration, or research may lead along paths away from the 'New Traditions' of raku and post-fire, but it is, I believe, the work which should speak when traditions are in question.

SMOKE RESIST

Already mentioned are crazed slips and the copper halo effect, both of which resist the deposition of carbon. Another way of resisting smoke could be to use vitreous slips on part of a surface. Wrapping parts of the form in damp cloth or aluminium foil also works. Loosely-applied sections of clay which are struck off after the pot has cooled will sometimes leave unsmoked marks on work. Sandblasting part of a smoked surface is another method of achieving contrasts between smoked and unsmoked areas.

BLOWTORCHING

Reduction of the glazed surface can be carried out directly using a gas blowtorch. Areas of carbonization can also be altered by the application of heat from such a gun. Factors such as the type of fuel, the burner, distance from work, and duration of treatment will all affect the final result. The main danger is that the uneven heating caused by this treatment will shatter the work. Careful preheating is a good idea, and deft handling of the burner will lessen the chances of cracking.

CLEANING

If work has been heavily reduced in sawdust it is often covered with a layer of carbon which obscures glaze and engobes. This is best removed with a stiff brush or scouring pad. How much of this carbon to take off is obviously a decision made as the surface emerges during cleaning. Soaking the work in water for a while may loosen stubborn carbon, and I have noticed that work which has been quenched on removal from the kiln is easier to clean.

Fig 28 Kazuo Yagi, 'Distance', blackfired (*photo: courtesy Ceramic Review*)

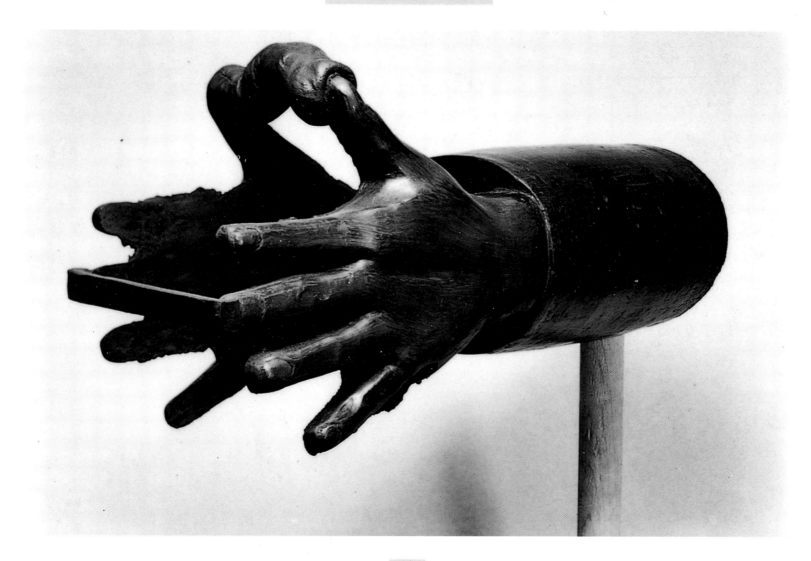

CHAPTER FOUR

RAKU KILNS

Choosing a kiln to fire raku work is a matter for heart and head. Each type of kiln will perform in a different way, have advantages and disadvantages when it comes to heating, packing, and withdrawing work. The qualities of glazes may be subtly or profoundly different according to the type of fuel, and to whether the work is oxidized or reduced during the firing. Choice of kiln will be dependent on the size and shape of the work, the space available for siting the kiln, preference for brick or fibre construction, and the availability of suitable fuel. This chapter will give you enough information to build and fire a number of different kilns.

BUILDING A PROPANE-FIRED, CERAMIC-FIBRE KILN

This design of kiln is lightweight and portable; it can be handled easily during drawing out, and altered if necessary. The structure is made from expanded metal or weldmesh. Both sorts of mesh can be painted

Fig 29 Top-hat fibre kiln 26 in (66 cm) internal diameter

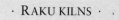

Paul Soldner, 1971, smoked white slip, iron oxide drawing, 16 in (40.5 cm)

with heat-resisting paint to give corrosion protection. Ceramic-fibre blanket is fixed to this framework by buttoning with fired clay buttons and Nichrome wire, thus making a very light and thermally-efficient heat box.

To make the structure you will need one sheet of 8 ft × 4 ft (244 cm × 122 cm) expanded steel mesh or weldmesh (choose a stock item, and one which is fairly easy to cut with tinsnips or wirecutters). Any size mesh will suffice if it is strong enough (see suppliers list). Ceramic-fibre blanket is available in different densities: I would suggest using the 8 lb (3.6 kg) high-density type. A roll of fibre will be sufficient to make two kilns. If at all possible work in a clear uncluttered space where there is good ventilation.

Use leather gloves when handling and cutting mesh, as cut metal edges can be sharp and can scratch. Measure out on your mesh the area which will form the sides of the kiln. For the small kiln, this would be approximately 60 in × 12 in (152 cm × 30 cm). Bend this into a circle and, using soft iron wire, or wire stripped from old electric cable, lace the mesh together, overlapping the joint, as in Fig 30. Now cut out another area approx. 21 in sq. (53 cm sq.) which will form the roof. Place this on top of the sides and, checking that the wall is still as circular as possible, mark out the circle of the kiln wall onto the top sheet with a felt-tipped pen or chalk.

Next cut the sheet roughly circular, allowing about 2 in (5 cm) over the kiln

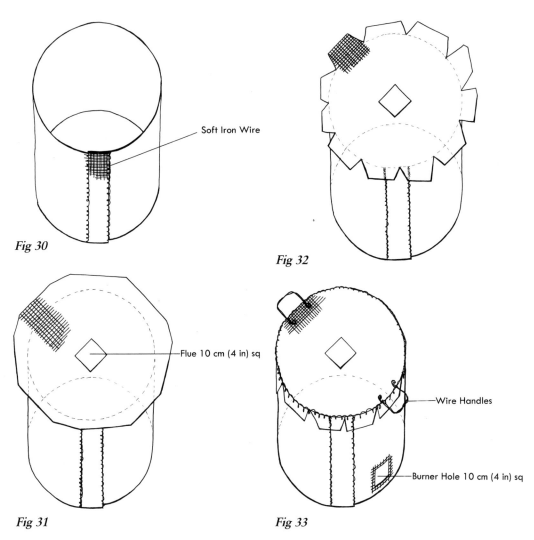

Fig 30

Soft Iron Wire

Fig 32

Flue 10 cm (4 in) sq

Fig 31

Wire Handles

Burner Hole 10 cm (4 in) sq

Fig 33

diameter (*Fig 31*). In order to fold the roof mesh down over the walls, cut darts out of the mesh (*Fig 32*), and fold down the edges by hand. Lace the top and sides together with wire, thus forming the 'top hat'. The flue hole in the top and the burner hole in the side can now be cut (*Fig 33*).

The base for the kiln could be simply two layers of fibre laid on housebricks, but for a more portable, less easily damaged base, mesh can be formed into a simple tray structure in which the fibre can rest. Cut out an area of mesh approx. 35 in sq. (89 cm sq.), snip out the corners (*Fig 34*) and fold up the edges. A length of wood may be used to form the 90 degree angle. The tray can then be laced at the corners. The base is deliberately larger than is actually needed for the small kiln because it can then be used for a bigger 'top hat'. If you have bought an 8 ft × 4 ft (244 cm × 122 cm) sheet of mesh and a roll of fibre you will have enough material to make another larger kiln, which could be switched over during firing with the smaller one, thus saving fuel and space.

Ceramic fibre can be bought as stiff board, in blanket form, or even in preformed shapes. It is normally white, not unlike fibreglass insulation in appearance, and is able to withstand high temperatures. The lining of the kiln is best completed outdoors because ceramic fibre releases some particles when handled. These can be an irritant to skin, nose, and throat. The best plan is to wear a mask and gloves and to work in the open air.

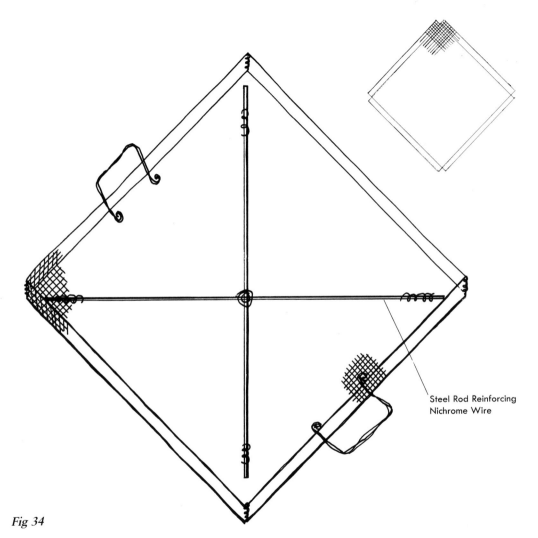

Steel Rod Reinforcing
Nichrome Wire

Fig 34

In addition to the fibre, you need to purchase about 79 in (2 m) of Nichrome wire or small-gauge Kanthal element wire, and to make 20 ceramic buttons. The buttons are simply squashed out from balls of grogged clay, pierced with two holes, and biscuit-fired to 1000°C (1832°F).

To measure the fibre for the cage, unroll a length of the blanket and, using the cage as a marker, press lightly with the upturned cage on an area. Cut a circle from the fibre which is about 4 in (10 cm) bigger than the imprint in diameter. This disc of fibre blanket is bigger than the cage so that it can be tucked into the corners, providing an overlap between the wall and roof (*Fig 35*). The wall

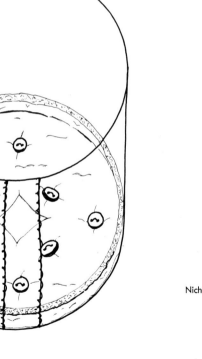

Fig 35

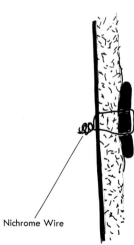

Nichrome Wire

Fig 36

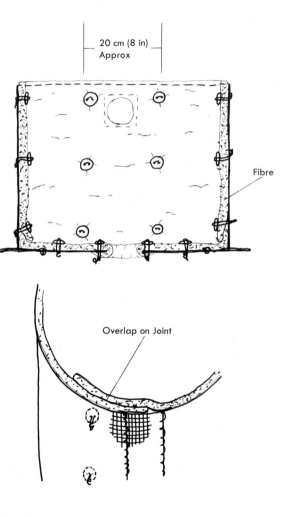

20 cm (8 in) Approx

Fibre

Overlap on Joint

Ian Byers, 'Opening Form', 1987, lustre glazes, max. dimension 7 in (18 cm) (photo: Pete Macertich)

of the kiln may also be marked out with the cage by rolling it along the blanket; because of the thickness of the fibre, the length needed will be less than the circumference of the cage. If you cut about 4 in (10 cm) less in length you will still have an ample overlap to provide a good heat seal. To complete the cutting of fibre, now cut out two squares to fit the base tray. All the cutting and trimming of fibre can be done with a pair of scissors.

Buttoning or fixing the fibre to the frame is a simple task. Cut lengths of the Nichrome wire so that they are long enough to pass through the button, the fibre and cage, and can then be twisted to form a firm fixing. The twisted ends should be bent over to render them safe. The spacing of the buttons should be roughly every 8 in (20 cm), and extra buttons must be used on the seams and to secure the fibre around the flue and burner holes (*Fig 36*). The base of the kiln does not need buttoning. This system can be used for virtually any size of kiln, but if firings are going to be much above 1040°C (1904°F), Kanthal wire will last longer. Thicker use of

the fibre would also be necessary for higher-temperature work.

The basic kiln that you have made can be added to, allowing taller work to be fired. You can use a circle of fibre surrounded by bricks as a quick temporary collar, or make a permanent extension collar using the same

technique as when building the kiln (*Fig 37*). The permanent option gives you an instant kiln change, and even a two-collar kiln is quite feasible for very tall work, with some thought about extra burners for an even distribution of heat (*Fig 38*). Having a larger base enables you to switch from small work

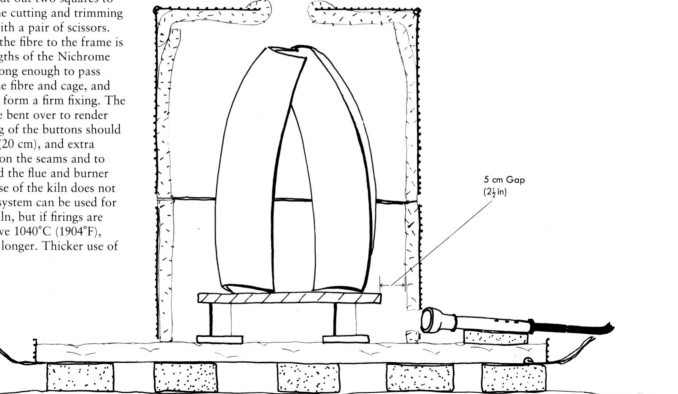

5 cm Gap
(2½ in)

Fig 37

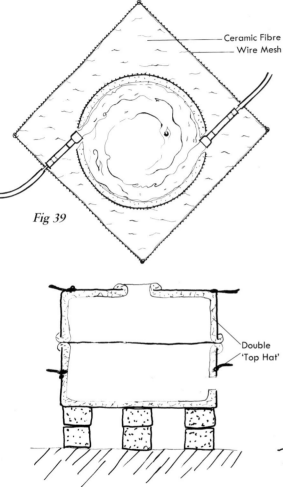

Fig 39

to large, or vice versa. If your work is unavoidably near to the roof of your kiln, and in particular the flue hole, you may have a cool spot on the piece, stopping the glaze melting at that point. The addition of a short chimney collar will often solve this problem, and simple handles, made from soft iron wire, can be added to the kiln and its base to make handling easy (*Fig 39*).

OIL DRUM KILN

An old oil drum can be used as an alternative structure to mesh for making fibre kilns. The disadvantages are that the steel drum needs to be weld cut, thus requiring access to more complex skills and technology. However, that said, the resulting kilns made in this way function well and have been used for a number of years in Britain and in the U.S.A.

The basic idea is to cut away the base, burner hole, and spyhole, from an empty oil drum and then to glue ceramic fibre to the inside with a special cement, purchasable from the fibre manufacturers. The cutting and overlapping of joints is the same as for the mesh kiln, and the same 8 lb (3.6 kg) blanket is used. The drum must be absolutely clean to enable the cement to stick, and to this end sandblasting and steam cleaning are the best

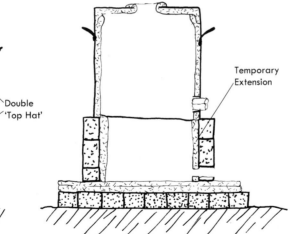

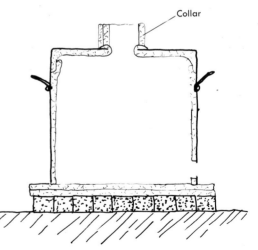

Fig 38

options. Of course the fibre could be fixed
with ceramic buttons and this would mean
drilling small holes for the Kanthal or
Nichrome wire. The cement used for fixing is
very sticky, so all the pieces of the blanket
should be tried in the drum for fit before
pasting.

The roof is pasted first and the fibre gently
stuck on with hand pressure. The sides are
then glued in, allowing an overlap which can
be carried over the edge and stuck to the
outside. Finally wire is bound around the
fibre on the outside to ensure firm fixing. The
holes in the blanket for burner hole, flue, and
spyhole are now cut, and the flaps poked
through and glued to the outside.

The kiln shown in Fig 41 uses a 45 gal
(204 l) drum and would need 5 in (127 mm)
flue and burner holes, and a 4 in (102 mm)
spyhole. The kiln is shown using bricks and
fibre for a base, but these could be substituted
for a base made from a cut-down oil drum
lined with fibre to form an insulated tray.
The kiln can either be fitted with simple
welded or bolted handles, or larger versions
could be lifted clear of work by a
counterbalanced pulley system, wires being
attached by the means of three eyebolts,
bolted through the top of the drum (Fig 41).
The wire or chain fixings to the drum are
protected from the heat of the flue gases by
three insulating bricks with a small kiln shelf
placed on top. Counterbalancing can be
achieved with another drum weighted with
sand or water.

Fig 40 *Small top-hat fibre kiln*

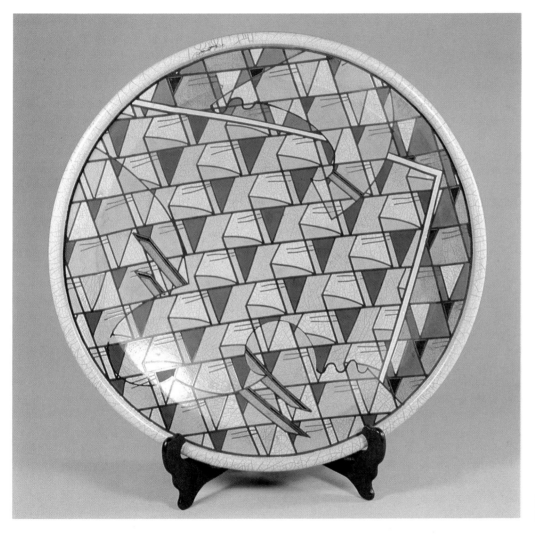

*Deborah Monaghan, platter dimension 20 in
(51 cm)*

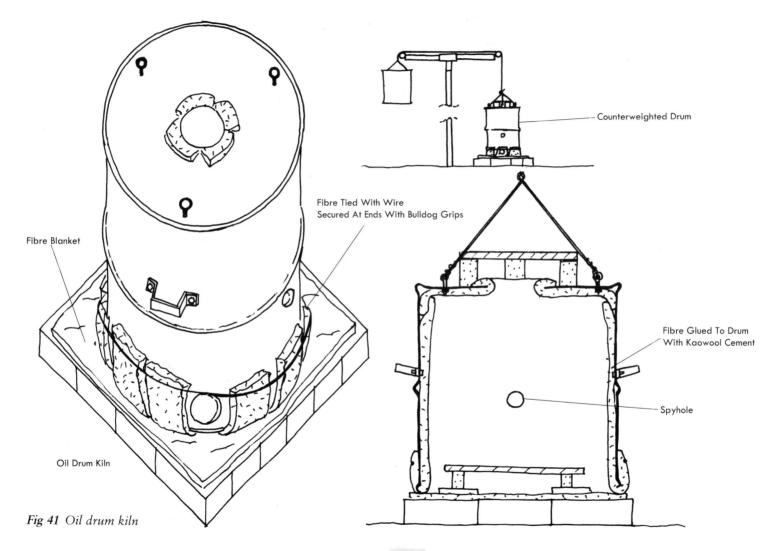

Counterweighted Drum

Fibre Tied With Wire
Secured At Ends With Bulldog Grips

Fibre Blanket

Fibre Glued To Drum
With Kaowool Cement

Spyhole

Oil Drum Kiln

Fig 41 *Oil drum kiln*

SMALL PROPANE BRICK-BUILT KILN

This kiln uses lightweight hotface insulating bricks for its structure and is similar to my first raku kiln (*Fig 42*). Insulating bricks are extremely lightweight, with excellent thermal insulation properties, enabling kilns to be fired quickly. The advantage over fibre is that work can be leant against the walls of the kiln without damage to the structure. Kilns made with bricks radiate heat to the work when hot, thus effecting smooth melting of glazes. As insulating bricks are sawn to size they do not need mortar between joints for raku work, and thus the kiln is completely demountable and can be stored as a pile of bricks. Figure 43 shows the pattern of bricks for the first three layers of the structure, with the maximum overlapping of joints for strength.

If the kiln is to be built as a demountable, the site must be levelled first with sand. A layer of housebricks is useful for keeping the insulating bricks dry. Insulating brick is soft and easy to cut with a pruning saw. By the time the structure reaches the fourth course of bricks they can be simply overlapped on the previous course's joints, until the full height of the kiln is reached. The height of the kiln can be adjusted for different heights of work merely by adding more layers of bricks. A very simple and effective lid can be made for this kiln with metal mesh, fibre, and buttons (*Fig 44*), or insulating bricks can be drilled and cramped together by means of threaded rods and angle iron, forming a sedan-type structure.

If a more permanent, portable kiln is required, the bricks can be stacked up inside an angle iron frame made up by bolting or welding to form a rigid structure which is transportable, either on wheels or in sedan fashion, using removable steel poles for lifting

Fig 42 *Propane-fired brick kiln, with counterweighted lid*

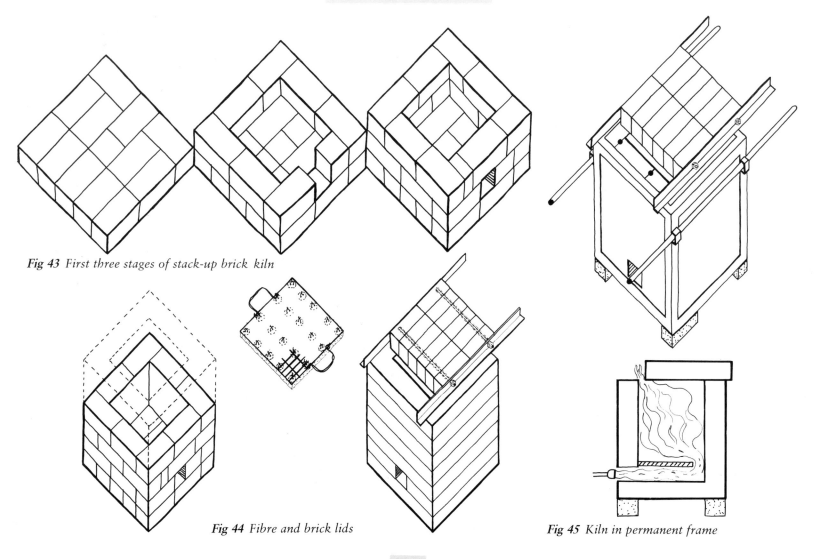

Fig 43 *First three stages of stack-up brick kiln*

Fig 44 *Fibre and brick lids*

Fig 45 *Kiln in permanent frame*

Wayne Higby, 'Fire, Rocks, Channel', 1982,
landscape bowl, height 11 in (28 cm)

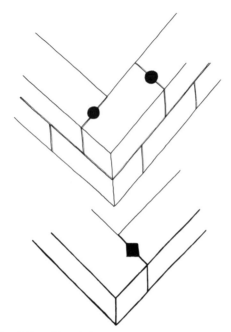

Fig 46 *Locking joint*

(*Fig 45*). A locking joint can be made by cutting out diamonds or circles of brick then filling the hole with aluminous cement plugs, for a more permanent solution (*Fig 46*). If the kiln is kept demountable, its shape can be changed or expanded to suit the size and shape of work. Additional burners may need to be used if the kiln grows in size, but the flame pattern can stay the same. More even heat is obtained using two smaller burners rather than one larger one.

STACK-UP BRICK KILN (SOLDNER TYPE) (*FIG 47*)

This kiln is based on the type used by Paul Soldner for workshop firings. It is quick and easy to build either with firebrick or, for a more fuel-efficient version, using hard brick for the base and to cantilever the arch bricks. This is a front-loading design and, as it is

Fig 47 *Soldner workshop kiln, for low fire, salt, etc.*

brick-built, can be used for low-fire salting. The kiln can be fired easily with two propane burners each delivering 75,000 bthu at 30 psi (see Fig 48 for corbelled arch and flamepath).

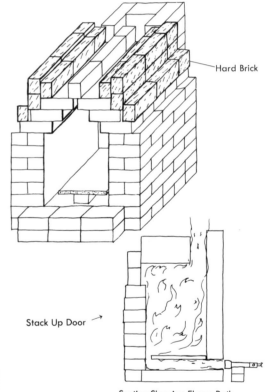

Hard Brick

Stack Up Door →

Section Showing Flame Path

Fig 48 *Stack-up kiln showing corbelled arch and flamepath*

SMALL TRADITIONAL RAKU WOOD KILN (*FIG 49*)

Thus kiln is similar to the wood muffle kilns used to fire traditional raku teabowls. It is built of hot face insulating bricks, and the wares are protected from direct flame by being placed inside a coarse fireclay/sand sagger. The structure is simply bricks stacked up to form the firebox and chamber on a levelled dry sand site. The muffle or sagger can be made by coiling and then bisque firing, normally to 1000°C (1832°F). Binding the clay muffle with soft iron wire will obviate any problems should the muffle crack during firing. The muffle is set on three bricks so that the flames from the firebox can pass under and around the muffle. Lining the lid with ceramic fibre will help to retain the heat within the muffle.

A spyhole in the lid enables the melting of the glazes to be glimpsed, and the work can be drawn out after the lid is removed with iron hooks or a bar passed through the loops on the lid. The kiln is most easily fired with pine splits $1\frac{1}{2}$ in × 14 in (4 cm × 36 cm) approx.

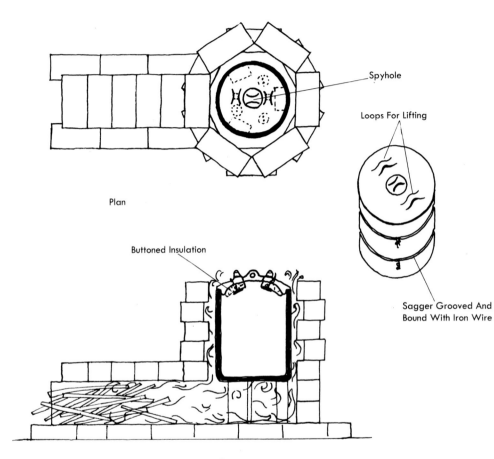

Plan

Spyhole

Loops For Lifting

Sagger Grooved And Bound With Iron Wire

Buttoned Insulation

Section Thro' Raku Muffle Kiln

Fig 49 *Traditional-type wood kiln*

CROSSDRAFT RAKU WOOD KILN (*FIG 50*)

This commonly-built design is quite sophisticated compared to the previous design. It can be built with about 250 ordinary housebricks or with hard firebrick. If firebrick is used, the whole kiln can be

Fig 50 *Crossdraft wood kiln*

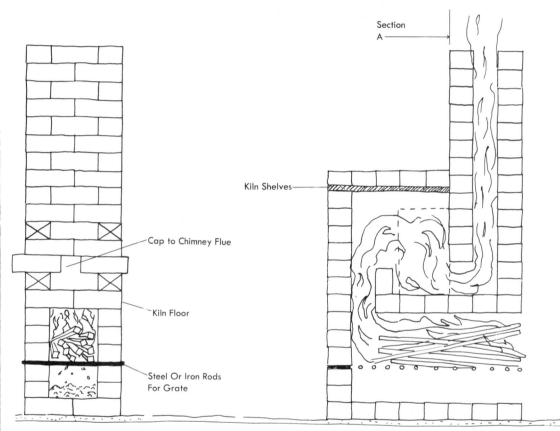

Cap to Chimney Flue

Kiln Floor

Steel Or Iron Rods For Grate

Kiln Shelves

Section A

Fig 51 *Section on chimney flue in direction of arrow A*

Fig 52 *Section through kiln showing flamepath*

Tim Proud, box, 1988

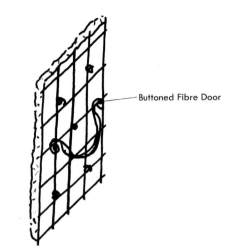

— Buttoned Fibre Door

— Half Brick

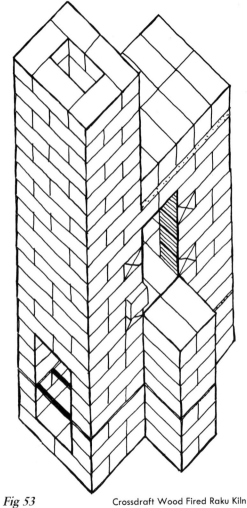

Fig 53   Crossdraft Wood Fired Raku Kiln

drystacked apart from the firebox course, which is laid into a clay and sand mix of two to one ratio. If housebricks of irregular size are used then a clay/sand slurry may be used as a mortar; this will enable the kiln to be demounted and the bricks easily cleaned. Although the kiln shown in Figs 51 and 52 has a kiln bat roof, the roof can be made by corbelling in like the roof in Fig 48; the whole structure could therefore be built of brick.

This kiln has an ashpit and firebars. The firebars should be either iron or steel, about $\frac{1}{2}$ in (13 mm) in diameter, and spaced at 3 in (76 mm) intervals. It is important to maintain an air passage between the bars and the ashes and embers which fall through. Failure to do so will result in the bars buckling and bending as the heat builds up. Like the muffle kiln, dry softwood splits, but this time cut to

2 in × 20 in (51 mm × 508 mm) will give an efficient heat rise. A simple fibre door provides easy access, and pots may be preheated on the roof of the kiln before firing. If you use the kiln for bisque firing whilst raising the kiln to working temperature, then placing shards carefully around the work will ensure the unfired work does not explode on contact with direct flame.

Both of the wood kilns can be fired with a weed burner gun. The latter can have its ashpit filled with bricks to reduce the area of combustion. The heat rise from this type of gun is quite fast so I would not recommend trying to bisque fire with this method.

A simple oil burner (*see Fig 56*) can also be used to fire both kilns, and the directions for its use are described in the section on burners.

TOP-LOADING ELECTRIC KILN ADAPTED FOR RAKU

Raku and electric kilns do not readily combine, but this idea by Jerry. J. Caplan (*Fig 54*) solves some of the problems in an intelligent way and could be useful to people working with raku who have top-loading kilns in a suitable position. Touching a live

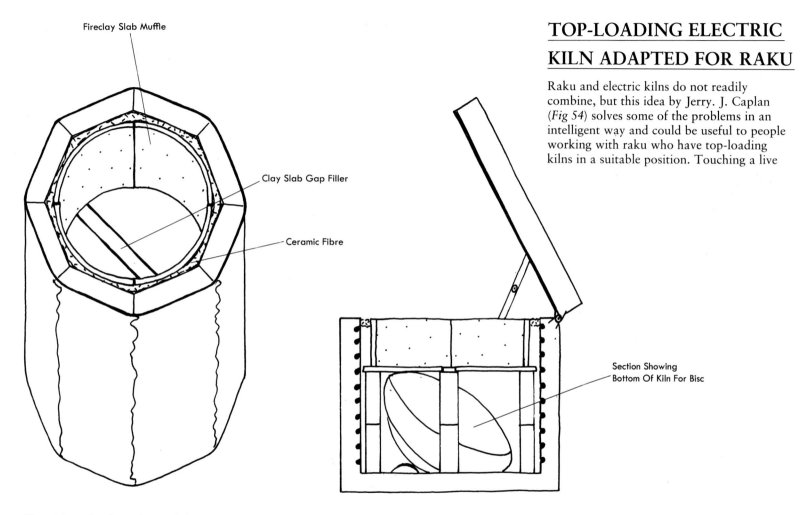

Fireclay Slab Muffle

Clay Slab Gap Filler

Ceramic Fibre

Section Showing Bottom Of Kiln For Bisc

Fig 54 *Top-loading electric kiln adapted for raku*

element with raku tongs could give a fatal shock; by creating a muffle wall between the elements and work this design obviates the tong hazard, and could be applied to other shaped top-loading kilns. Electric-fired raku is very clean, very oxidized, unless reduction material is introduced into the muffle, and the glazes can be melted swiftly and evenly. By blocking off the elements, the design cuts down the thermal shock which operates each time the lid is removed and which would reduce the element life of a normal electric kiln. I would recommend this type of kiln if access to outdoors was immediately adjacent and easy; I would never work indoors because of the fire and fume hazard. However, if all the necessary contingencies were met, this kiln could be a useful tool.

Electric kilns adapted in this way, if controlled by switches and/or Sunvic regulators, should be turned off before work is drawn out for safety reasons. Kilns using a kiln sitter system can be fired with an 06 cone (Orton) and raku work drawn out while the kiln is still climbing. Turning the power down would also extend the period of time that raku can be fired. A nice feature of this kiln is that bisque work can be set in the lower part of the kiln, thus combining raku and bisque in one firing and also making the kiln less deep for retrieval of pieces.

The clay slabs forming the muffle walls can be made from two parts fireclay to one to three parts sand mix. The thickness of the slabs could be just over $\frac{1}{2}$ in (12 mm), and if they are made to fit the kiln when plastic, the fired size will leave a suitable gap between elements and muffle which can most easily be filled with a thin strip of ceramic-fibre blanket.

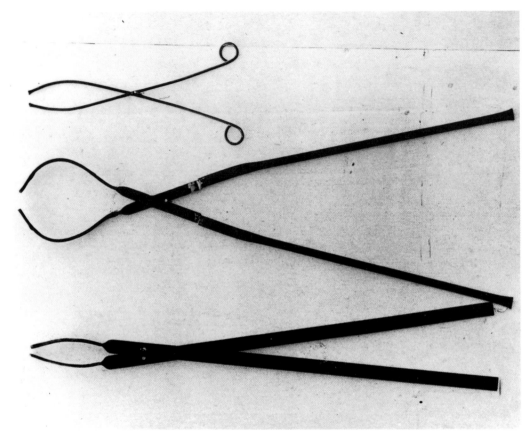

Fig 55 Raku tongs made by Ian Byers, maximum dimension 39 in (99 cm)

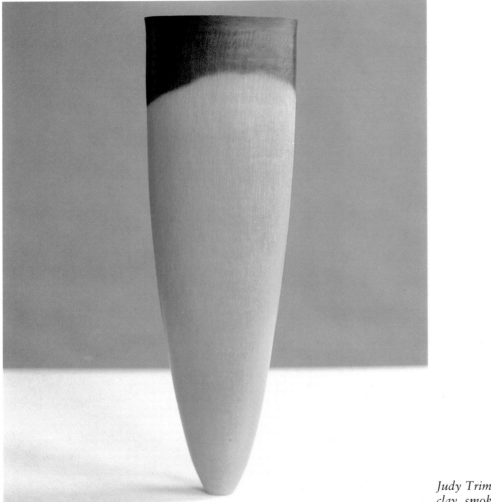

Judy Trim, oval beaker, 1985, burnished red clay, smoked (photo: Bryan Rybolt)

CHAPTER FIVE

FUEL, BURNERS AND FIRING

PROPANE

Both brick and fibre kilns are quick and easy to fire using liquefied petroleum gas and a suitable burner. Propane rather than butane is normally used in Britain. Propane gas in a liquefied form is purchased in refillable bottles of various sizes. A 42 lb (19 kg) bottle is easily moved around and will give many hours of firing if used with the fibre kilns described. Liquefied gas evaporates as the gas in the bottle is drawn off. A high-pressure regulator controls the pressure of the gas being supplied to the burner. Apart from the burner, the hose, clips, and regulator can be obtained from a gas dealer. The manufacturers of burners are usually only too pleased to advise on the matching of burner type to your requirements for a particular kiln, and I would turn to them in cases of difficulty.

Liquid gas as a fuel is clean, efficient, and easily transported, but like any flammable material it needs care and sensible following of safe procedures of use. Propane is heavier than air, so if there is a gas leak, it could flow down into drains or basements, etc. where it could explode. I would always fire outside, undercover if necessary, but in an open space where any gases or smoke can disperse easily. Here is a simple procedure to follow when firing.

1. Check all joints for gas leakage with soapy water before starting to fire; never use a flame!

2. Always turn off the bottle valve first when opening or shutting down the gas supply.

3. When preparing to light the burner, open the valve on the top of the cylinder, then gradually screw down the tap on the pressure regulator, until gas is heard at the burner tip. Light the burner before offering it up to the burner port.

4. When shutting down the burner, first turn off the gas at the cylinder, then unscrew the tap on the regulator, and withdraw the burner from the kiln.

Arrange any hoses, bottles, and other equipment such as tongs so that they are clear of the kiln, the space where the kiln will be placed during loading and unloading, and the reduction area.

PROPANE BURNERS

I have tried various makes and also made my own, all of which proved adequate. Probably the cheapest solution is to buy a burner gun (*Fig 56*) which incorporates its own control valve; however, these can be tiresomely noisy and are not particularly efficient. The burners that I now use are efficient and quiet, even if two are being used together. (See list of suppliers on p. 93.) A burner which is able to supply 77000 bthu of heat would easily fire a fibre or hot-face insulating brick kiln of 3.46 cu. ft (0.098 cu. m) capacity.

OIL AS A FUEL

Kerosene (paraffin), central heating oil, and waste oil are all widely available. Kerosene and heating oils are thin and easy for forced-air burners to atomise, and thus burn

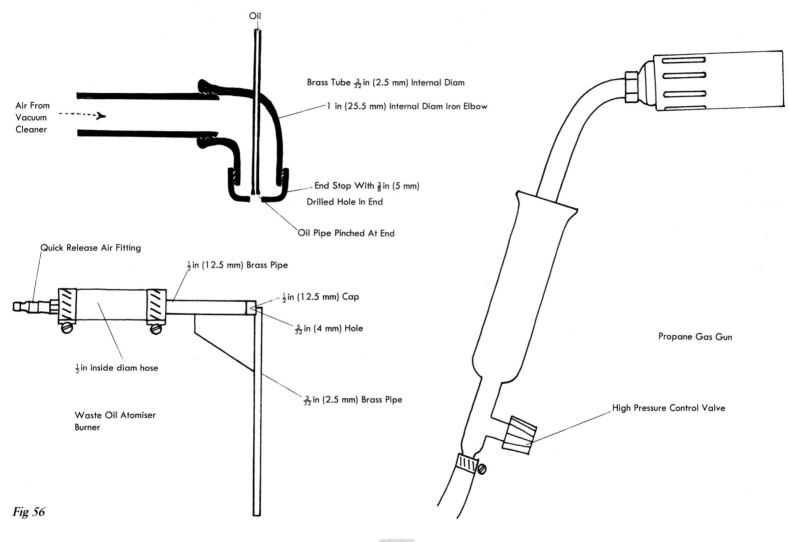

Oil

Air From
Vacuum
Cleaner

Brass Tube $\frac{3}{32}$ in (2.5 mm) Internal Diam

1 in (25.5 mm) Internal Diam Iron Elbow

End Stop With $\frac{3}{8}$ in (5 mm)
Drilled Hole In End

Oil Pipe Pinched At End

Quick Release Air Fitting

$\frac{1}{2}$ in (12.5 mm) Brass Pipe

$\frac{1}{2}$ in (12.5 mm) Cap

$\frac{5}{32}$ in (4 mm) Hole

$\frac{3}{32}$ in (2.5 mm) Brass Pipe

$\frac{1}{2}$ in inside diam hose

Waste Oil Atomiser
Burner

Propane Gas Gun

High Pressure Control Valve

Fig 56

efficiently, whereas waste oil is very thick and requires a cruder atomiser. Waste oil is difficult to burn efficiently at low temperatures, and if it is to be used can be mixed with a thinner oil or used later on in the firing. Oil is highly inflammable, and kilns operating with forced-air oil burners should never be left unattended, and should incorporate a solenoid cut-out valve in the oil system in case of blower failure or electric cuts. Regulations regarding the siting of drums and oil tanks should be carefully noted and adhered to and all oil equipment sited clear of the unloading or reduction areas.

FORCED-AIR BURNERS

Although it is possible to buy very efficient and expensive oil burners, quite simple and reasonably efficient burners can be made using gas pipe or standard plumber's pipe fittings. The gravity-fed burner shown in Fig 56 uses a tubular vacuum cleaner as its forced-air source, and the oil (kerosene or paraffin) is atomised by the action of the blown air meeting the fine spurt of oil from the burner tip. The adjustment to the air pressure is effected by bleeding off air from the vacuum through a sliding vent in the air supply tube. The oil supply is pressurized by raising the tank of drum to create a head pressure. This type of burner gives a large heat output and a long flame and has been used for large kilns. The burner could be used to fire the two wood-burning kilns, starting the firing with wood then transferring to oil

on red heat. The burner is kept lit below red heat by the means of a target brick placed in the path of the flame, which, once glowing, will relight the burner.

FORCED-AIR BURNER USING WASTE OIL

The burner designed by Tom Morissey and shown in Fig 56 is similar to an art fixative spray: oil is drawn up the vertical pipe from a simple can reservoir of oil, when compressed air from a small compressor is blown across the top of the tube. The burner can handle either waste oil, a mixture of waste oil and paraffin, or paraffin only. Kilns using sump oil as a starting fuel can be very smokey, but used once the kiln is hot, waste oil, which is often available free, can be used fairly cleanly. The burner is positioned in the can by cutting a small notch in the edge in which the burner rests. It is important to insulate the oil reservoir from heat from the burner port. This can be achieved by placing it behind an insulating brick. The burner could be used to fire any of the wood brick kilns illustrated.

Oil, as compared to gas, needs more space to burn, and if you change from gas burners to oil, a larger firebox space should be allowed in kiln design (see Frederick Olsen's *The kiln book* p. 107). The two homemade burners described are known as low-pressure burners, and need roughly 1 sq. ft (0.09 sq. m) of combustion space for every 5 sq. ft (0.46 sq. m) of kiln floor area.

WEED BURNER GUN

This type of burner is normally used for burning off grass and weeds, but it can be used to fire raku kilns. The burner is fed from a tank of kerosene (paraffin), which is pressurized by hand pumping. The gun will supply ample heat to fire a small raku kiln, but careful filtering of fuel is often necessary to avoid injectors blocking.

WOOD AS A FUEL

Firing a kiln with wood requires energy and skill. Only very dry wood will give a good heat release. Fresh felled timber will need to be dried out for a year to be an efficient fuel, as any water in the wood will form steam as combustion takes place, thus negating heat release. If scrap timber is available, however, this can be used immediately. The size of timber is also crucial. Large logs have a relatively smaller surface area than small-diameter splits and therefore burn more slowly than the thinner fuel. When raising the temperature of a raku wood kiln, thinner sections of wood are best, and, as the firing progresses and the kiln through-draft increases, the stoking rate can also be increased. Softwood, because it is less dense than hardwood, burns more quickly, effecting a more sudden heat release. When the kiln is hot, thin dry wood will literally explode into flame spontaneously giving a long but gentle flame through the kiln chamber. The key to firing with wood is to make the best of your

Ian Byers, shallow dish, 1986, coloured glazes, 15 × 12 in (38 × 30 cm), (photo: Pete Macertich)

own energy as well as that of the woods; it is important to have energy left over from preparation and stoking to apply to the work. Previous preparation of wood and division of labour between two people, one firing and the other stoking, is probably the best way of using wood as a fuel to fire raku.

FIRING

FIRING A TOP HAT FIBRE KILN WITH PROPANE

Firing kilns with propane gas is fairly simple, but there are some rules of thumb which will help you, until you get a feel for the process. Work to be fired is best set on a kiln shelf rather than bricks because this allows for good heat radiation to the piece. The shelf should be cut to the shape of the kiln but be roughly 4 in (10 cm) smaller in diameter to allow free flow of flame upwards. If the kiln has a fibre base, it is important to spread the weight of the kiln props resting on it. This can be done by placing small pieces of broken shelf under each. The shelf may crack after several firings, in which case merely support it with more props.

The next stage is up to you but, personally, I dislike firing too many pots at once. My reason is that control over cooling rates and over reduction is lost when trying to cope with numbers. It is also important that the work does not block or throttle the flow of gases through the flue exit. The effect of this would be to stop the kiln rising in

temperature. Any work that is biscuit-fired, glazed, and completely dry may be set on the shelf ready to fire. It is most important that the water taken on by the biscuitware during glazing is evaporated off, as this is the most frequent cause of work exploding during the firing.

Once the work has been set and the 'top hat' positioned on the base, you are ready to light the burner and proceed. The burner should be placed so that it creates a flame which will flow around the kiln. This helps with even heat distribution. If two burners are being used, they should be arranged alternately (*see Fig 39*). Using a pyrometer for the first firing will help you to judge the rate at which you can increase the gas pressure to achieve a steady rise in temperature. Trying to increase the pressure too quickly will cause an arresting of heat rise and a reduction atmosphere in the kiln. Ideally there should be a small flame showing at the flue exit, which shows that the kiln is filled with flame. Judging the optimum heat rise for your work is obviously a case of trial and error, some shapes will survive well no matter how they are treated, whereas others will need careful heating and cooling. The variations are enormous, but after a while personal conclusions can be drawn about what will survive the rigours of heating and cooling. My approach is to have few preconceptions, but to try it and see; the results are often surprising, for instance slipcast work often survives well.

As the firing progresses, the walls, shelves, and work will begin to glow. Some raku glazes will boil vigorously as they begin to melt out, whilst others very quietly melt into a smooth surface. It is important to fire glazes with the same melting and maturing range together in the kiln, otherwise the glaze on some work will be boiling and uneven, when others are fully mature. An aid to looking at the surface of pots is to shine the light from either a torch or a mirror into the kiln so that the surface of the work can be seen clearly. A fully-melted glaze will shine and show an evenly-melted surface free from bubbles. Direct flame from a badly-positioned burner can cause boiling and bubbling which will not disappear easily. The important thing is to watch the glaze through its stages of maturation and, once the surface is melting out, to turn the burner back, and soak the glaze at its top temperature.

Once you are satisfied that your work is ready to draw out, follow the burner shut-down procedure. Lifting the kiln off its base reveals the piece and gives you the chance finally to check the glaze surface, continue firing if necessary, or to remove the top hat to a safe spot. Remember that this part of the kiln is very hot, so place it on a surface which will not be damaged.

RAKU WOOD-FIRED KILNS

The effects of heat are obviously the same with different types of wood and kilns, but some additional points are worth considering.

Positioning the firebox in the direction of the prevailing wind will assist the draft through the kiln and thus speed temperature rise. The two kilns shown can reach working temperature in one and a half to two hours if conditions are favourable. It is also important to pack the work in the kiln in such a way as to allow flame passage through the ware and flue, and to look out for cool spots to ensure good results.

OXIDIZING AND REDUCING IN THE KILN

When flames from burning oil, wood, or gas have a good supply of air they burn up the carbon in the fuel to produce heat and carbon dioxide. If there is enough air mixing and burning within the flame, almost complete combustion can be achieved. This is known as an oxidizing atmosphere in the kiln. When a kiln is oxidizing, the objects inside can be seen fairly clearly. If the flames are starved of air, unburnt carbon in the firing chamber will make visibility poor, and glazed surfaces will appear indistinct making it difficult to gauge their stage of melting. Heavy smoke may appear from spyholes and chimneys and through cracks in the kiln's structure. Raku work fired with oil, gas, or wood will never be completely oxidized in the way that work fired in electric kilns is. Firing with fuels that will easily produce reduction atmospheres can therefore be a way of working which adds the in-kiln reduction effects to those obtained by post-firing treatments.

Obtaining a reduction atmosphere with oil and gas burners is fairly easy and can be achieved in two ways: by restricting the primary air to the burner, or by damping the flow of gases through the kiln. Gas burners usually have a slide or primary air vent on the burner which can be partially closed, thus producing an inefficient flame. Forced-air oil burners will produce a reducing flame if the air supply is insufficient or if too much fuel is released through the fuel jet. Kiln damping is achieved by building in a sliding vent to the chimney flue, or more simply by covering part of the chimney or flue exit with a piece of kiln shelf. In-kiln reduction in wood-fired kilns can be achieved by over-stoking. The effect of reduction is also to slow temperature rise or even to produce a fall in temperature.

Starving the kiln of oxygen affects glaze colour. Metallic colouring oxides such as copper oxide are robbed of some or all of their oxygen, depending on how heavy the reduction is. An alkaline glaze containing copper will turn red or even metallic copper colour if reduced, rather than the typical turquoise of ancient Egyptian or Turkish glazed wares. This colour change often penetrates the whole depth of the glaze, unlike the reds and metallic colours obtained from copper in post-firing treatments. Certainly in-kiln reduction and the effects of differing fuels on reduction and glaze quality are not to be ignored.

CHAPTER SIX

PERSONAL APPROACHES

Working with fire

flames   spread

   understanding

CHRISTINE CONSTANT

Christine Constant worked in stoneware and earthenware till five years ago. She writes of the difference thus:

I had a fear of using glazes in standard earthenware/stoneware firings, in that I would make endless tests and decisions, put glaze all over the object, like a glossy cover, and then be upset by the separateness of the glaze to the article's surface. I didn't feel like this when I used raku. I felt happy to paint on different glazes in different ways, and less inhibited by the glazing process which became more a part of the form.

The traditional Japanese version of raku has not influenced her own developments; in fact, she says

Fig 57 Christine Constant, untitled, 1989, raku-fired

I rather think I probably misuse the idea, i.e. exercise too much control and worry abut it, so I feel that I am not very much in tune with the original philosophy. However I would imagine that the qualities which so excite, delight and draw me would be similar.

Christine's understanding of the term includes 'simplicity, wholeness and spontaneity, in art, as in life', but in a more practical vein she says

The term to me mostly means a crucial moment taking work out of the kiln, and I really have to lock in all my mental and physical energy to get it right. This may seem over-dramatic, but if I lose my nerve or concentration, I lose the piece. I never have that feeling when I'm just doing a task, like packing a kiln, wedging up clay, etc, and I always feel emotional about firing, be it giddy or tense.

Other activities inform her raku work or exist as parallel activities:

I sketch ideas about shape, and I draw and play with colour, surface, texture, and form,

Christine Constant, 'Embedded Husk', 1988

less than I would like to, I take a great deal of photographs of images, patterns, surfaces, and forms that interest me. Often the photographs will have a distinct time element in them, i.e. the lighting conditions of that particular moment conspire with me to make certain patterns of connections. This is in addition to being a recording device, is what interests me about photography. It's cheating, you can take a record of the moment and place home. I also collect quirky or scrap items, which seem to have some affiliation to me or my work.

Christine's work and attitudes have changed considerably from the early work's hard, precise, sharp surfaces, and flat stable glazes, to a more moody 'organic, geological, dark feel', which uses more variable glazes to obtain, 'lustrous, glistening surfaces' (*see page 75*). Her time is divided between 'teaching and making'. In regard to her making, she follows her own inclinations, although if market demands start to impinge in an obvious way, she tries to bring herself back to 'source'. On a practical level her work is often partly hand-built, partly slipcast, and uses a variety of clays: 'T' material, semi-porcelain, or white earthenware with molochite added for whiteness. She fires her work in a counterweighted fibre kiln, preferring to work alone or with a friend 'who knows the way I work'. Firing may go on for a day with four or five pieces, treating one at a time because,

'the correct moment for one is not the same for the other'. Finally, raku, she says, has changed the way she approaches other work.' I find I can apply the same uninhibited approach to other things.'

DAVE ROBERTS

Mao Tse Tung said 'Let the past serve the future'. Dave Roberts' links with history are something he calmly accepts: 'I don't see any problems with the fact that what you do, somebody else has done 2000 years ago. It's quite reassuring really.'* Dave has done much to publicize raku in Britain through his participation in workshops and demonstrations, and also through the imposing scale of his work. Size and physicality are important elements of his pots, and he finds the challenge of making large pieces a great stimulus. Their scale also lifts them out of the ordinary scale of pottery in general, which can be contained in your own personal space. These pots work by assuredly occupying *your* space, as well as their own.

The large, simple, soft, egg-like forms of his bottles sometimes display elements of Chinese ceramics, such as the fatness of the glaze quality or the vestigial handles. The handles serve to extend an action or movement, or to reinforce a constriction, the major 'actions' of the pot being the container and the opening. The openings or necks seem to be there to tap in, or funnel out, elements,

as well as to create a tighter, contrasting, circumflexed movement. The low temperature of his work enables the forms to retain intact, without subjection or submission to the elements of distortion and slumping, which are ever-present hazards for high-fired work, where allowances such as thickening of sections have to be made.

By removing himself from functionalism and utilitarian work, Dave has found an area where he is free to explore his own subject matter which he describes as 'dealing with universal concerns of form, order, proportion and harmony'* under the cloak of the decorative object. Working with clay sorted out his subject matter, which was always a problem in regard to his earlier painting experience. He says of this experience 'As soon as I started working in clay, the actual material took over, and it didn't matter about the subject anymore'.* The subject matter of his work seems to have a reasonably large audience, and could possibly provide his entire income, but he prefers a balance of working and teaching. He sees himself making 'decorative' arts and working for a luxury market, and is content within this definition. He includes photography, reading, and visiting museums under visual research activity.

During the development of his own particular version of raku, Dave has avoided contact with Japanese raku, but he concedes that 'Modernist ideas, and the aesthetic context in which I work, has I suspect been

Dave Roberts, large coil-built bottle, 20 in (52 cm) high

influenced by Zen philosophy, e.g. less is more'. He thinks that raku is now, 'so fragmented, that it only makes sense in relation to the individual's interpretation, and development of the ideas, and processes associated with raku'. His own definitions would include, 'drawing pots from the kiln and then doing something to them'. His control over glaze and surface is taken to an extreme; he says that he would like 'as much control as possible', over firing and post-firing, and 'I think with a lot of inherently accidental firing processes (salt, lustre, etc) you have to have as much control as possible'. This desire to exert control is, however, 'softened by the raku.'*

Dave's work is even-sectioned and round – factors which he finds help avoid the stresses of thrown or slabbed work. However, there are still some losses which he tries to view with detachment. His work is fired in top-hat fibre kilns, and then post-fire reduced in purpose-made steel bins, the work being allowed to cool for two hours before removal. Recipes for one of Dave's slips is included in the chapter on slips and glazes, p. 35.

Raku may, in the future, influence his approach to other work, as he is 'considering applying fast and flexible firing processes to high temperature work'.

*Quotes from interview with Steven Brayne, *Ceramic Review*, No 105.

DAVID MILLER

David Miller lives and works in France, where he supports himself on a mixed economy of domestic stonewares and more individual one-off raku fired pieces which follow his own inclinations, without concern for fashion. He became interested in raku through contact with Jim Romberg, an American raku potter. David became known in Britain through his low-fire salt work. The work from this period used a language of multiple thrown forms, distortion, and calligraphic surface marks, along with all the variability of copper slips and salt. More recently he added post-fire reduction effects to the salt, and now concentrates on effects obtainable through raku and post-fire reduction.

David's work is informed and developed by process, in conjunction with drawing which he uses to liberate ideas through the simplicity of the contact between head, heart, brush, and paper. He says 'as an idea changes and becomes tangible, drawing serves as a stepping stone, enabling me to solve both visual, and technical problems'. David Miller's work, like Paul Soldner's, employs asymmetric balance of form, texture and calligraphic mark. Carrying the composition to the kiln and through to post-firing is also a Soldner trait, but although David Miller's work inherits an approach, its activity is completely different. There is a homely, down to earth nature in the work, now coupled

Fig 58 David Miller, *vase form, height 10 in (25.4 cm)*

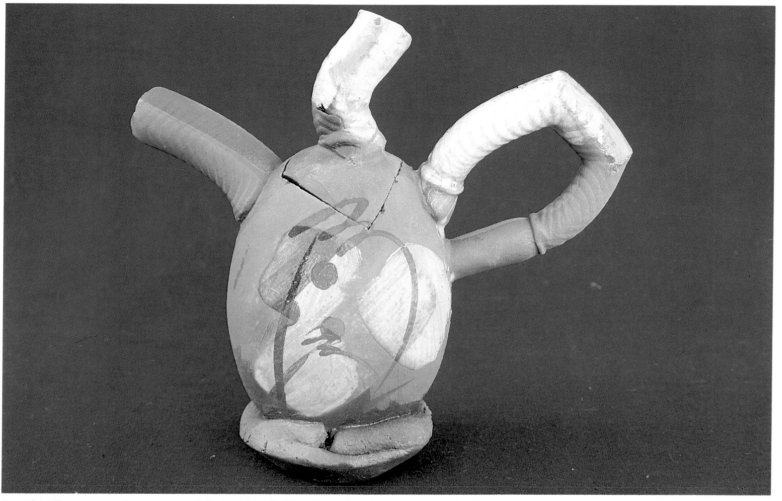

David Miller, teapot, thrown, remodelled with rolled handle and spout, 8 in (20 cm) high

with a sense of humour (*see pages 35, 78 and 79*). He says of his recent work 'I am excited by the colour and contrast, combined with the humorous imagery that I feel is developing in my work'. This humour is aimed in all directions – at himself, the teapot, and to the viewer. The heavy squashed coils, parodying handles and spouts, express the primal quality of the clay media, whilst at the same time conveying the supposed delicacy and sometimes absurd ritual of some of life's activities.

David's knowledge of traditional raku is sparse, perhaps deliberately so. 'This philosophy is far from my understanding, and therefore, far from my reasons for making Raku.' Having developed his own direction, he admits that he is 'now interested to know something about its history'. Like many raku potters working alone, some concentration is vital to his work. But, interestingly, he does say that, 'working in a group, (teaching, demonstrating etc), unexpected things can happen, which I benefit from at a later date'.

On a practical level his work is now fired in a oil-fired top-hat fibre kiln. As he uses 'little or no glaze on my work, the pieces can touch each other. This allows for a fairly dense pack, so depending on size I can fire between ten and twenty pieces in one session. I like to group pieces usually in three's, which are fired together.' When post-fire reducing work, he places pots in beds of sawdust and 'precisely placed pieces of newspaper, to create areas of more intense reduction'. This

importantly produces 'intermittent waves of reduction and oxidation'. The reduction is carried out in metal bins, sealed with fibre lids, and pots are left to cool in these until they can be touched. His recent work uses glazes, engobes, and stains fixed with a small amount of frit, effects which resist smoke, and create haloes around marks and colours. Amongst David's aims for his work is the wish for his pots 'to have the same quality as drawings: spontaneity, freedom etc.'.

WAYNE HIGBY

Wayne Higby's recent work is a play, a space where visual elements constantly disrupt expectations of space or ideas of composition (*see pages 59 and 81*). The work is fluid, it flows through spaces both real and expected, in an extra-perspective, unfocusing way. Our inability to contain the work brings forward sensing-knowing, rather than the intellectually comprehending act. It is a now-you-have-it now-you-don't experience, augmented by richness of surface and the knowledge that what you are looking at is still pottery and strong within that identity.

ARTIST'S STATEMENT, OCTOBER 1988

Is reality a state of mind or a physical condition? 'Both' I would say.

My ceramic work stands as a testament to such an answer. Material presence and

mental image find common ground in the pot as landscape theme.

I am concerned with landscape imagery as a focal point of imagery vision not as a representation of a particular location. Space both real and implied, is of utmost importance. I strive to establish a zone of quiet coherence – a place full of silent empty space where finite and infinite, intimate and immense intersect. This goal is achieved through a rhythmical connecting and reconnecting of physical structure with illusion.

The fusion of opposites is the underlying thesis upon which my work is based. Form–surface, sculpture–painting, fine art–applied art are but a few of the polarities I seek to bridge. A thoughtful look at each piece will reveal numerous ways in which a part–counterpart relationship brings depth and subtlety.

The chance of the raku fire is a complementary opposite to the precision I use in constructing form and surface. More importantly, in relationship to landscape imagery, raku is a process of firing which affords a ceramic route to the illusionistic reproduction of natural light and shade.

At first, raku seemed to provide a more intimate and immediate way of working than other ceramic techniques. Now, I realize that my original interest in raku stemmed primarily from an over excited desire to see results quickly. I soon outgrew a fascination with the serendipity of chance events. At least

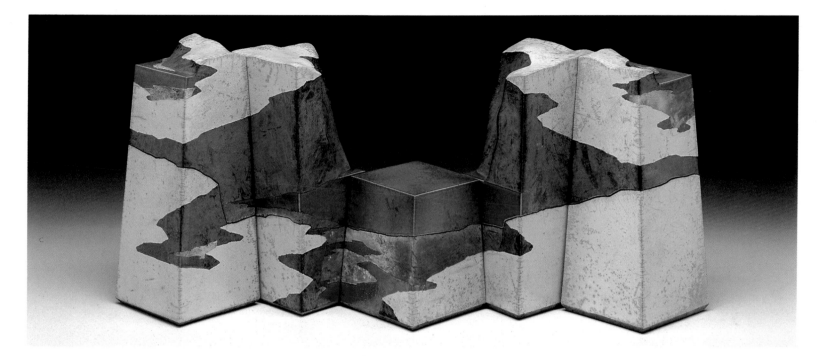

Wayne Higby, 'Symmetrical Days Landscape Container', 1982. Five boxes with lids, 31½ in (80 cm) wide

to the point that chance and surprise were seen as an end in themselves. I wanted a stronger concept. Moving on to other techniques, I began to intuit ways of putting chance to work. Eventually, I returned full-time to raku when my interest in landscape began to focus a direction. The facet of my artistic instinct which I call the painter – one who uses glaze and fire – realised that the effects of light could be captured via raku's unique reduction phenomena.

I don't believe that every step an artist takes on the road to a finished statement must be enjoyable. Some steps are boring, some are tedious, and others often physically exhausting as well as dangerous. I have often considered never making another raku pot.

The process becomes more difficult as I raise the stakes and the risks too great to each individual piece (some of which take a week or more to make). Be that as it may, I am held by the qualities of the finished object as it is delivered out of the filth and stench of the reduction material to stand as a confirmation of a personal reality mindful of the firing process and its entrapment of light and shade.

MAILA KLEMETTINEN

Maila Klemettinen, a Finnish artist, practises raku in a cold climate. She sometimes fires her work outdoors when the temperature is $-20°C$ ($-4°F$). Much of her work has been figurative sculptures made in stoneware, but more recently her work has been raku-fired, and post-fired reduced. She says, 'I think that raku suits the forms and atmosphere of my work'. The decision to raku fire may come only after a piece has been made in a normal stoneware body, so there can be considerable risk involved in firing, but if the work requires it, she raku-fires anyway.

The suggestive powers of the process have become more important of late, and much of her recent work has moved toward 'more abstract expression'. It is the ability of the object to evoke a mood or project emotion that is central to her choice of raku firings (*see right and opposite*). The power of the work can often be derived from the raku acts of chance, which sometimes free ideas or relationships at an unconscious level. Although she may use glaze on only one area of the surface, the glaze can be a catalyst allowing a shift or a slip of meaning away from the explicit. Her work does not seek to find answers: it creates a situation which calls for reaction.

Ideas for work are caught in sketchbooks she carries 'constantly', and are put down as 'a small sketch, perhaps with a note of colour and the meaning' (to her) of the piece. Some

of her recent titles for work have included, 'A Fortress, Sarcophagi, Big Tower, and Visions' – the title being a touchstone for her, the viewer, and the piece.

Fig 59 Maila Klementinen, 'A Fortress', 1986, raku, height $15\frac{3}{4}$ in (40 cm) (photo: Seppo Hilpo)

Maila Klemetinen, 'A Woman Riding a Lion', 16 in (40 cm) high (photo: Seppo Hilpo)

GRETCHEN WACHS

Gretchen Wachs is an American potter/vessel-maker living and working in New Mexico. She can work all year round with raku, varying her firing cycle to the length of day. Gretchen is able to support herself through the sale of her ceramic work and prints, which are shown together. These two activities overlap and provide inspiration and ideas for each other. One of the things that excites her about this relationship is using three-dimensional form to express what she has been doing with colour and design. Working with clay, engobe, and glaze also allows for a wide spectrum of textures and wet and dry surfaces. Although she is represented by a number of galleries and committed to producing a certain volume and consistency of work for her 'market', she considers it very important to continue to explore new ideas. She says 'The most important thing is that my work continues to develop, and for that to happen, I need time in the studio making art for its own sake, and not for the gallery. Eventually it will end up there but in its own time.'

STATEMENT OF PURPOSE

I've just taken a load of pieces out of the raku kiln. I sit for a spell to recover from the frenzy of that activity; the contact with that degree of heat, and the weight and volume of the pieces. Layered with wet clothing, and to

Gretchen Wachs, 'Figurative Construction', 1987, 27 in (58 cm) high

protect against the heat, I am a mixture of exhaustion and relief of having gotten the pots out of the kiln and into the reduction chamber, without dropping one on my toe or setting myself on fire. I wonder sometimes if its worth it – the crackle and the smoked surfaces – but it's more than that. I would feel somehow estranged if I didn't have this intimate contact with the work one last time, at this crucial stage of development.

I will have a look at the pots in another half hour or so. They will still be hot, but possible to handle with gloves. I will see for the first time since I painted them – shiny wet-like surfaces and colours matured. Much of the ceramic work relates directly to the figure, but often the imagery on the torso-like forms is more abstract. I paint the clay forms when they are green and soft, and anything can happen. For me, it's at this stage that the work takes off.

The monotype prints and my ceramic work are synergistic. Both processes lend themselves well to the way I work. I choose the monotype process in part because of the immediacy of it, and also because of that element of chance that, as in raku, is inherent in that process. It is not entirely in my hands; when the plate emerges from the press and I see the print, image reversed, ink transferred in ways I couldn't have predicted, it is somewhat the same feeling as when I pull the ceramic from the oil drum, to see how smoke and fire have altered my best laid plans.

That is the magic . . .

JILL CROWLEY

Jill Crowley first became involved with raku as a student at the Royal College of Art in 1969. This involvement was 'partly as a way of being completely independent and partly through the support, both technical and moral which she received from John Dickerson, whom she sought out, and who allowed her to fire teabowls in his kiln. Teabowls grew into teapots and a visit to Paul Soldner's workshop in Aspen in 1972 has resulted in her being hooked ever since'.

Jill Crowley's vision has mostly been of the particular, rather than the general. Cat heads, portrait heads with pocked and bubbling skin, torsos, hands, and feet all come under her scrutiny and imagination, as sometimes humorous, sometimes grotesque, yet sharply-focused fragments of life (*see page 86*). Her work seems to be concerned with peripheral vision – the glimpses of life which we could easily exclude because they are not always beautiful or easy. At their best they are penetrating. Jill's portrait heads never had a sitter, yet in their presence we may feel that we know just such a person. Her 'unknown portraits' of hands and feet bulge or wriggle in an excess of humanity, and make you look more critically, more warily, at your own.

Not all of her work is raku, in fact there have been times when sudden inspiration turned the subject in view from soft raku to hard stoneware. Raku has so far drawn her back, to its 'complete balance of form and

Fig 60 *Jill Crowley, 'Lady', 1982, 14 in (36 cm) high*

surface', sometimes to frenetically finish a show's work in just a few days. Another way that raku works for her is that it allows her to evolve a series of images quickly and expel the rush of ideas. Ideas are not so much the problem as that of selecting the best ideas; realizing and selecting the important ones from that rush is the critical act. There is always the slightly unnerving sensation after meeting Jill that part of you might just turn up as part of one of her developments, in rather greater detail than you might wish.

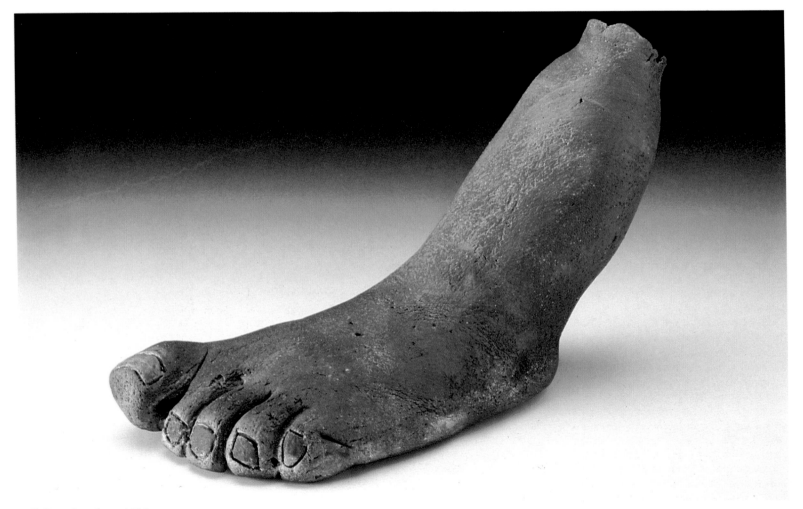

Jill Crowley, foot, 1986

RICHARD HIRSCH

For me, raku is an attitude, a way of thinking and working. It is not a firing process nor a technique. My pieces are conceived as raku long before their introduction to fire. They are a reflection of what I think the definition of raku is.

Initially my tripod vessels draw aesthetic sustenance from and try to make meaningful connections with archaic vessel traditions. While these vessels continue to retain the fundamental anatomy of pottery they are devised as abstractions. It is my intention that they be perceived as functionally inaccessible and formally scuptural, yet purposefully contained in vessel architecture. Some pieces are about exaggerated mass and physical and visual weight. In others, the forms are skeletal in nature and include a compacted-core volume as centre. Space and line are emphasised rather than mass. The colour palette is a subdued patination leaving the impression of antiquity. This element is juxtaposed against the contemporary sensibility of forms.

In the series entitled Vessel and Stand (Coper Metti Series – *Fig 23*) scale is physically diminutive and the vessels are deliberately elongated. Their presentation on a tripod stand pursues the feeling of ceremony and develops a monumentality beyond their true dimensions. By purposely raising the pieces of this type of pedestal I give visual praise to the vessel as an art form.

Richard Hirssch, Coper Metti series, green-orange sigillatas, cupric sulphate spray, 1986–87, 19 in (47 cm) high

ITSUE ITO

Itsue Ito no longer makes raku work. Her experience of raku was initially that of 'fascination with the spontaneousness of the process'. Working with raku first in Japan, then in the States, she began seeking to unify both cultural influences in her work. Making raku work in the USA began to open up her means of expression, from 'the obvious starkness of the surface of Japanese culture' through to the 'freedom from tradition which the States offered'. Her work now involves the synthesis and interplay of the two cultures. Her present theme, that of 'Man and Nature', seems to have been present in her raku work where organic elements were held together within a formal framework. Within her present work, man, the viewer, is free to roam amongst the clouds and landscape on her work, yet the formality remains. She says

Conceptually the nature of sky became my starting point and the emotions that exist in dreams followed. The endless numbers of colours that exist in sky with their graduations of tone represent dreams and dominate the design of my pieces. Though natural beauty and dream are impossible to duplicate, I attempt to express a harmony rather than duplicate natural phenomena throughout my work.

Itsue's raku work employed sparing use of organic colours, and it was not until she saw the beautiful tiles of the Rushtempasha Camii

in Istanbul that she became alive to the possibilities of colour (low-temperature high-alkaline vivid blues in particular). Her present work is still low-fired with commercial glazes and lustres and assembled after all the firings are complete.

Fig 61 Itsue Ito, Dialogue 3, 1983, handbuilt, low-fired clay, bisque stains, epoxy lustre, raku-fired, 29 in (73.6 cm) wide (photo: George Erml, courtesy American Crafts Council)

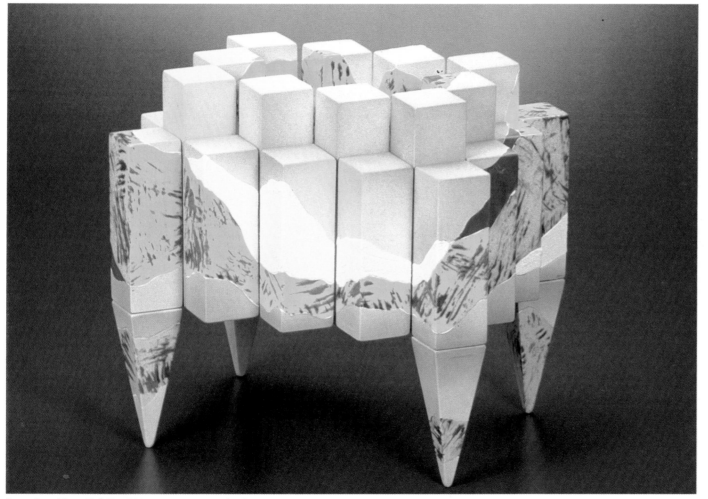

Itsue Ito, 'San Geki', 1989, 12 in (31 cm) high

CHAPTER SEVEN

RAKU . . . DOES IT EXIST?

The raku 'butterfly'[1] has developed from a specific, traditional base, into the wide-ranging 'bird'[1] of modern attitudes and practises. For some it still means a direct involvement in firing, whilst others use it as part of their art, without any particular attachment. Soldner's reassessment of raku refers directly to the original meaning of the word 'freedom or comfort', and to someone like Nureyev as being a raku dancer. The decision of what it is, or what it is not, it seems in the West, at least, is now open to the individual's own assessment and response.

Whilst attending a Japanese conference on raku, Paul Soldner was told unceremoniously that 'Americans couldn't make raku, because the Emperor didn't give us the right'.[2] The utterer of these words, the present Mr Raku, was right, in Japanese terms, and in some ways this statement lets us off the hook. Soldner did, however, point out that the word was there before the ware. People in Japan today still invite people to their homes to be raku – in 'freedom' or 'comfort'. Soldner's own answer to the dilemma was simple and funny: Ukar . . . a word with similar qualities but perhaps having the reverse effect. Raku is a word with definition; Ukar is still being defined, and so is open-ended.

One key element of recent raku and post-firings is that of chance. This element of the activity goes against the grain somewhat, for most of our lives we expend energy and a great deal of thought avoiding such occurrences. Happenings outside our control are repellent to the ordered mind. It is also not surprising that chance is not a major factor in our lives. We try to regulate everything because chance is dangerous and we have in the past had to protect ourselves from it. Man's ability to cope with chance occurrences has also been of crucial importance to his material, physical, and mental progress. Being in league with chance is not easy – in fact it becomes more and more difficult as we raise our standards. As the area of raku and post-firings becomes wider and more well defined, so we may find that 'we'll just go to certain points in it, points with which we are already familiar',[3] raku, too, has its own traps, which we must constantly reassess. To work with risk and chance we must, in a way, empty the pool of our expectations if we are to succeed.

We often bring to the work preconceptions about how something should be, and it is only in the doing that the work develops a life and rules of its own, which, if we allow, can open up new avenues of thought and exploration. Raku is good at challenging our assumptions of how a work should be because of the variables involved in its production. This does not set Raku apart from other temperatures or methods of firing, but the unique personal involvement with the work that raku offers can lead to a more instinctive way of working.

Although I have ideas, draw, etc. before going into the studio, it is not until I start, perhaps working on a piece in hand, that I start to know what the next work will be about. It is a conscious/unconscious, intellectual versus intuitive reaction. Once the work begins to speak, preconceptions can be laid aside and the real work begins. Sometimes this can mean laying aside raku, or even clay. Clay for me, however, is something special, which allows for sense of touch, directness of expression, and emergence of thoughts and feelings undiscovered. Allowing these feelings to surface is the aim, and the involvement with raku, in addition to direct contact with the work at all stages, also helps to release elements of the work as yet unknown.

If what we are aiming to do is to work against our expectations and conscious seekings, we may find that we are out on our own, faced with what Eric Fromm called 'the anguish of choice' and relying entirely on our own decisions and efforts. Making work in this way may mean picking up on visual ideas which we may at first have rejected or denied because they were unfamiliar. There may also be tensions involved in the production of work, and this again could seem at first to be wrong or unfamiliar; but it is also quite natural and as it should be.

A balance of control/lack of control is often necessary to avoid contriving. I have often found that the best work has come out of a situation where my own abilities to control the medium are stretched to the brink. Perhaps collaboration is the best word for the working process – a give and take situation, rather than the conscious manipulation which repetition can bring. The pressures to repeat or conform are always there, and perhaps we are living in a society which doesn't value the special qualities of art, or take the view that they are the result of risk-taking.

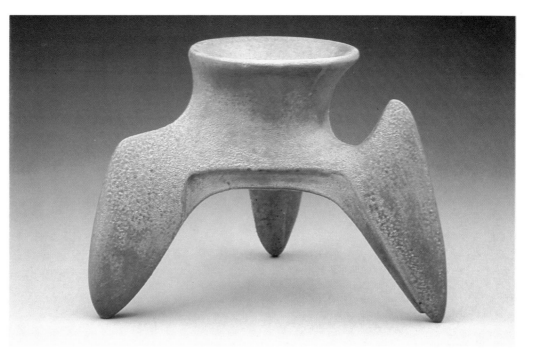

Richard Hirsch, blue-green terra sigillatas, low-fire glazes, 1985–85, 12 in (31 cm) high

As artists, potters, ceramists, vessel-makers – call ourselves what we will – we are living in a world faced with great environmental and social problems, a world of overproduction and overconsumption. It is in this context that we are all making works, and the future development of work which involves risk and close involvement with process, call it raku if you like, will ultimately be judged on its own merits to be good or bad.

[1] Quoted by Raku-san, at a slide presentation of American Raku given by Richard Hirsch in Kyoto, 1978.
[2] Paul Soldner, *San Francisco Examiner*. Nov 9, 1980.
[3] John Cage, Calvin Tomkins, *Ahead of The Game*. Penguin, 1965.

GLOSSARY

Biscuitware Ware fired previous to glazing.

Blunger Machine for mixing slips in bulk.

Bthu British Thermal Units.

Calcite Crystalline form of calcium carbonate.

Colemanite Natural source of boron (can be substituted by gerstley borate).

Engobe Slip containing glaze materials, which is usually more vitreous than the body it covers.

Feldspathic High in feldspars, (50% or more of glaze recipe).

Grog Fired then crushed ceramic, used to produce more open-textured clay.

Kanthal High-temperature element wire.

Levigate Suspend particles in a liquid.

Molochite Calcined china clay grog.

Nichrome wire Nickel/chrome element wire.

Pinholing Small smooth-edged hole in fired glaze surface.

Sagger Fired clay box used to protect wares in kiln from direct flame.

Shards Broken pieces of fired ceramic.

Spodumene Lithium flux used as a body addition to give thermal shock resistance.

Nepheline syenite Feldspar high in sodium and potassium.

Post-firing reduction Reducing work in sawdust etc. after removal from the kiln.

Weldmesh Metal lathing.

SUPPLIERS

CLAYS

U.K.

Potclays Ltd, Brickkiln Lane, Etruria, Stoke on Trent.

English China Clays, John Keay House, St Austell, Cornwall, PL25 4JD. (Molochite)

Morgan Refractories Ltd, Liverpool Road, Neston, South Wirral, Cheshire L64 3RE ('T' Material).

Acme Marls Ltd, Bournes Bank, Burslem, Stoke on Trent ST6 3DW. (Fireclays)

FRANCE

A.G.S., Clerac, 17270, Montguyou, Charente Maritime.

U.S.A.

A.R.T. studio clay Illinois.

COLOURS STAINS AND FRITS

U.K.

Ferro GB Ltd, Ceramics Div, Nile Street, Burslem, Stoke on Trent, ST6 2BQ.

Potterycrafts Ltd, Campbell Road, Shelton, Stoke on Trent.

FRANCE

Sifraco, 11, Rue de Teheran, 75008, Paris.

GERMANY

Degussa, Postf, 110533, 6000 Frankfurt 11.

KILNS

Stack away raku kilns
John Gooding and Roger Watts, Pearsons Green, Brenchley, Tonbridge, Kent.

CERAMIC FIBRE AND KILN BRICKS

Ceramtech 3, Brampton Sidings, Hempstalls Lane, Newcastle, Staffs. (Fibre blanket 6 or 8 lb high-density).

Molar, Hythe Works, Colchester (Hotface insulating bricks MPK LW25).

PROPANE GAS BURNERS AND EQUIPMENT

Aeromatic Barter Ltd, Kynoch Road, Eley's Estate, Edmonton, London, M18 3BH. (One FR1 No 50, Drill No 62 will fire 3 cu ft kiln. For larger kilns use two or FR 1 No 75)

METAL MESH

Weldmesh, Downhills Steels, Uxbridge, (1 in soft colour) or any steel mesh stockist.

SUBSTITUTE MATERIALS U.K./U.S.A.

U.K.	U.S.A.
High-alkaline frits	Ferro 3110 984°C Ferro 3124 1031°C
Standard borax frit	Ferro 3134 Pemco P–54
Calcium borate frit P2954 (Potterycrafts Ltd)	Gerstley borate Colemanite
Lead bisilicate frit Lead sesqisilicate frit	Ferro 3489 Ferro 210701 (Great Britain, available in the USA)
Cornish stone, China stone	Cornwall stone; Caroline stone, Kona A–3; Pyrophyllite
Feldspar (potash)	Bell, Buckingham G–200; Kingman K–200; Custer
Feldspar (Soda)	Spruce pine 4; Kona F–4
Fremington red clay	'Albany' type clay
Zirconium silicate (Zircon)	Zircopax, Opax

SELECTED BIBLIOGRAPHY

Dickerson, John. *Raku Handbook*. Studio Vista. London; Van Nostrand Reinhold, New York, 1972.

Earl, Joe (Ed.). *Japanese Art and Design* (The Toshiba Gallery), Victoria & Albert Museum, London, 1986.

Gablic, Suzi. *Has Modernism Failed?* Thames and Hudson Ltd, London, 1985.

Goldman, Eric. *The Crucial Decade and After*. Vintage Books, New York, 1975.

Leach, Bernard. *A Potter's Book*. Faber and Faber, London, 1973.

Leach, Bernard. *Kenzan and His Tradition*. Faber and Faber, 1973.

Nigrosh, Leon. *Lowfire*. Days Publication, 1980.

Okakura, Kakuzo. *The Book of Tea*. Dover Publications, New York, 1964.

Olsen, Fred. *The Kiln Book*. Keramos Books, California, 1973.

Rosenberg, Harold. *The Tradition of The New*. Grove Press, New York.

Stryk, Lucien and Ikemoto, Takashi. *The Penguin Book of Zen Poetry*. Great Britain, 1981.

Tomkins, Calvin. *Ahead of The Game*. Penguin, Great Britain, 1968.

Tyler, Christopher, and Hirsh, Richard. *Raku*. Watson Guptill, New York, 1981.

Wechsler, Susan. *Lowfire Ceramics*. Watson Guptill, 1981.

MAGAZINES AND PERIODICALS

Chanoyu Quarterly. Urasenke Foundation, Kyoto, Japan.

American Crafts (formerly *Craft Horizons*). American Crafts Council, 40 W. 53rd Street, New York 10019.

Ceramics Monthly. Professional Publications, Inc. Box 12448, Columbus, Ohio, 43212, U.S.A.

Ceramic Review. 21 Carnaby Street, London, W1.

INDEX